A PARENT'S GUIDE TO PUBLIC EDUCATION IN THE 21ST CENTURY

NAVIGATING EDUCATION REFORM TO GET THE BEST EDUCATION FOR MY CHILD

A PARENT'S GUIDE TO PUBLIC EDUCATION IN THE 21ST CENTURY

NAVIGATING EDUCATION REFORM TO GET THE BEST EDUCATION FOR MY CHILD

RUSS WALSH

GARN PRESS

NEW YORK,NY

Published by Garn Press, LLC
New York, NY
www.garnpress.com

Book and cover design by Benjamin J. Taylor/Garn Press

Library of Congress Control Number: 2015960372

Publisher's Cataloging-in-Publication Data

Names: Walsh, Russ.
Title: A parent's guide to public education in the 21st century : navigating education reform to get the best education for my child / Russ Walsh.
Description: Includes bibliographical references.
Identifiers: LCCN 2015960372 | ISBN 978-1-942146-33-9 (pbk.) | ISBN 978-1-942146-34-6 (ebook)
Subjects: LCSH: Education--Parent participation. | Educational change--United States--Citizen participation. | Public schools--United States. | Privatization in education. | Charter schools--United States. | BISAC: EDUCATION / Educational Policy & Reform / General. | EDUCATION / Parent Participation. | EDUCATION / Aims & Objectives. | POLITICAL SCIENCE / Public Policy / Cultural Policy.
Classification: LCC LA217.2 .W35 2016 (print) | LCC LA217.2 (ebook) | DDC 371.01/0973--dc23

For my mother, Virginia Haman Walsh, who read to me, and my father, William J. Walsh, Jr., who taught me the importance of showing up and speaking up.

Table of Contents

How to Read this Book

The book is set up in a question–answer format. I try to ask the questions that parents might ask and provide clear answers to those questions from the standpoint of being a parent and grandparent myself, as well as being a public education advocate. The Table of Contents lists each of the questions that I have posed and attempted to answer. Readers may wish to direct their reading to a particular chapter or to a particular question of interest within a chapter, like "Do charter schools do a better job of educating children than traditional public schools?" (Chapter 11), or "Should I opt out of standardized tests for my child?" (Chapter 10), or "What kinds of progress in literacy should I see from my child over time?" (Chapter 4). Reading in this manner may prove to be the most efficient way to use the book and might also lead to other questions that can be answered elsewhere in the text.

The first chapter of the book focuses on the history, the driving concerns and the players in 21st century education reform. This chapter provides an overview of the issues that will be discussed later in the book. The chapter also provides the framework that informs the rest of the book. While it is not necessary to read this chapter to get answers to your main questions, it does provide a context for all that comes after.

Chapters 2 through 6 are concerned with your role as a parent, your children as learners, and advice on getting the best education for your children. In these chapters I will look at what makes a good school, how to be sure your child is ready for school and how to make sure the school is ready for your child. I will discuss what good literacy and mathematics instruction looks like and how to know if your child is progressing appropriately. Whether your child attends a traditional public school, a charter school, a private school or is home-schooled, these chapters provide guidance on providing the best education for your own child.

Chapters 7 through 11 discuss the proposed solutions to the problems of public education that have been the chief focus of educational reform over the past 20 years. These chapters focus on getting quality teachers in the classroom, the Common Core State Standards, standardized testing, and school choice. Reading these chapters will help you to understand the current issues related to educational reform and how they are likely to impact you and your children and your children's children no matter what schools they attend in the future.

A Bill of Rights for School Children

It is clear that in the near future public education faces tremendous disruption and change. How this great American institution emerges from this change is of critical importance to every parent and child in the country. In the city of New Orleans, the system of public education as we have known it has been almost entirely replaced by a system of privately run, publicly funded charter schools. In other cities, like Philadelphia and Detroit, where adequate resources have long been denied to the public schools and where the public schools have been struggling for decades, more and more of the responsibility for educating the children has fallen to charter schools, both brick and mortar schools and cyber schools.

The current crop of education reformers argue that these changes are necessary, that the situation in many inner-city schools demands that we try something new. There is no question that something must be done to improve the quality of the learning experiences that children get in the inner cities. What the education reformers miss is that the public school system, any public school system, is both a reflection of and a product of the community where it resides. Reform cannot be focused on one element of that community, like the schools, and be successful.

We have seen that in the United States public schools in affluent areas consistently perform at a very high level. We see this in community after community, county after county, state after state, all across the country. Parent income is the single best predictor of student readiness for college and career. It is notable that in many of these affluent communities, teacher unions are strong and vocal, charter schools are virtually non-existent and test scores and every other measure of student learning are off the charts. Every one of these communities has both been able to and willing to make a financial commitment to quality public schools. Strong unions have not stood in the way of strong student learning. Teachers perform at a high level. Principals and other administrators are both qualified and highly engaged in producing quality learning.

It seems obvious that if we are going to improve public education in the economically struggling inner cities, we must take a holistic view. We must attack poverty with as much vigor and energy as the education reformers bring to their lobbying efforts in support of opening more charter schools. We must provide children in the inner cities with more services than schools in affluent areas because these children need more help to become proficient learners. This means wrap around services like medical and dental screenings, increased availability of counselors to help children navigate the trauma of their daily lives, home-school counselors that assist struggling families in providing experiences for their young children that will help them when they get to school, and professionally run and developmentally appropriate pre-school programs. All of these things will help and they will help much more than sending a child across town to a new charter school that has promised to raise student test scores.

Education reformers have it wrong. We cannot end poverty by improving educational opportunity. Education has proven a way out of poverty for a select few of course, but for most children, the debilitating impact of poverty cannot be overcome in the classroom.

To truly serve these children we must first concentrate on ending income inequity. If we can make significant strides in improving the economic outlook of the 24% of American children living in poverty, improved educational opportunity will be the joyous and very predictable outcome.

As we look to future, it may be useful to consider some principles about public education that, for me at least, seem immutable. A Bill of Rights for the school child if you will.

1. Every child has a right to a free, high quality, public education.

2. Every child has a right to attend a well-staffed, well-resourced, clean and safe local neighborhood school.

3. Every child has the right to be taught by well-informed, fully certified, fully engaged teachers who care about the child as a learner and as a person.

4. Every child has the right to a school that provides a rich and varied curriculum that includes the visual and performing arts, integrated technology, and physical education.

5. Every child has a right to a school that provides a rich and varied extra-curricular program including athletics, clubs, and service learning opportunities.

6. Every child has a right to instruction that is well-planned, engaging, and collaborative.

7. Every child has a right to instruction that is developmentally appropriate.

8. Every elementary school child has a right to daily recess.

9. Every child has the right to go to a school with adequate support personnel including librarians, nurses, guidance counselors, and learning support specialists.

10. Every child has a right to an element of choice in the educational program, including the right to choose to take advanced level courses.

As parents it is of course in our interest to see that all of these things are available to our own child, but it is also in every parent's interest to make sure that every child has this opportunity. The world that our children will inhabit in the future will be populated by an increasingly diverse citizenry. If we want the best that this country has to offer for our own children, we must work to ensure that every child in this country has similar opportunities. For our own children to reap the benefits of the American Dream, to live happily, freely and securely in the challenging world of the future, we must make sure that everyone's children have access to that same American Dream.

Introduction

> *Going to school is not the same as going shopping. Parents should not be burdened with locating a suitable school for their child. They should be able to take their child to the neighborhood public school as a matter of course and expect that it has well-educated teachers and a sound educational program.*[1]
>
> **Diane Ravitch**: *The Death and Life of the Great American School System: How Testing and Choice Are Undermining Education.*

In September 1953, I walked across the street from my house and into the John Fitch Elementary School, a public school in Levittown, PA, to begin the first grade. Sixty years later, I retired as a public school administrator from a school district in New Jersey. In between I attended a public junior high school, a public high school, and a state college. I then worked in a public high school, a public elementary school, a state college, and finally for a public school district. In the public schools I got an excellent education that prepared me not only for college and career, but more importantly, for life. In the state college I was well prepared for my chosen career as a teacher and had my interests in history, theater and good books nurtured. Working in the public schools, I got to fulfill my dreams of being a teacher and coach who impacted the lives (mostly for the better I hope) of hundreds of children. I even got to surprise myself later in my career by becoming a supervisor and being, as one second grade student called me, "the teachers' teacher."

My parents did not choose to send me to public school. They chose where they would make a home, primarily based on finding a place close to my dad's work that they could afford ($100 down and $87 a month) and sent me to the public schools because that was the only option they could afford or imagine. As a child the only school choice I knew of was to go to public school as I and virtually all of my friends did, or to go to the Catholic school across town, as my cousins did. My family was neither Catholic nor in a position to afford tuition, so public school was our "choice."

All three of my children attended public school because that was the best option for our family. All three also attended state supported colleges, again due to our choice and our family economics. Public education provided the keys to fulfillment for my children just as it had for me. My grandchildren are currently carrying on that tradition. They are fortunate to be in a school district with an adequate budget, a rich and varied curriculum with lots of effective teachers, and opportunities to pursue their interests in science, social studies, music, theater, dance and volleyball. America's system of public education has been very good to me and my family.

This book was written because I believe that every parent should have the "choice" my parents had and because I believe every child should have the chance I had. That is, the choice of a well-resourced, well-staffed, clean and safe neighborhood public school and the chance for an education that provides preparation for living a rich and fulfilling life.

This book was also written because this greatest of all American institutions, our system of public education, is under attack from the right and the left, from Republicans and Democrats, from wealthy individuals and well-funded non-profits, from newspapers, movies and television shows. It was written because public education is under attack from a free market ideology that failed Wall Street and will fail our children if left unchecked.

Finally, this book was written to provide parents, who are rightly seeking the best possible educational opportunities for their children, with guidance and clear-eyed thinking on the issues. In the face of a confusing narrative about failing schools and bad teachers what is a parent to think? Are public schools really that bad? What is the Common Core? What are the uses and abuses of standardized testing? Should I send my child to a charter school? Will vouchers provide my kids with a better shot at a good education? Just what is a parent to think of all this?

This book will not provide a fair and balanced, dispassionate look at these issues. The book is decidedly pro-public education and anti-corporate education reform. It is not a plea for a return to the good old days, but a guide for moving forward in a way that will help parents not only get the best education for their children, but also help them advocate for policies that will be good for the institution of public education.

All of us want the best for our own children, but what is best for the institution of public education is not only good for our own, but for everyone's, children. Whether we choose to send our children to a traditional public school, a charter school, a religious school or a private school, all of our children will have to live in the world that our education systems have created. Therefore, it is in the interest of all parents, and all taxpayers for that matter, to ensure that every child has access to the benefits of a vital, nurturing, edifying public school system.

Our children are our most precious gifts. We all want them to attend a school that provides a warm, nurturing, stimulating social, emotional and intellectual environment where they can learn and grow and pursue their own passions. Schools have a sacred trust to provide these things for our children. This book attempts to suggest ways that we can assure that our public schools meet this challenge and are worthy of this trust.

1

Education Reform in the 21st Century

What are the roots of education reform?

In one sense, reform is a constant in education. It is the professional obligation of all teachers to keep current on the research on teaching and learning and to integrate new understandings into their instruction. To a parent this can look like a dizzying cycle of confusing and sometimes contradictory practices. In reading instruction, for example, we may find that our school goes from a "look-say" approach, to a literature based approach, to a whole language approach, to a phonics based approach, to something called "balanced literacy." This can all be very disorienting, but for the most part these changes reflect attempts by professionals to reform their practice based on the best current available knowledge.

There is another kind of school reform, however, that is not driven by teachers, but by politicians and business people. This kind of reform has also been around since public education began, which is understandable because public education uses public funds. Public funds means taxes, which means, in turn, politics and money must enter into the educational equation. Citizens earn their right to voice opinions about public education by paying their taxes and politicians (at least theoretically) represent the citizens in the various state and federal offices.

The history of politically driven educational reform is fascinating, but beyond the scope of this book. Suffice it to say that education reform movements began as soon as public education began and that the players and the themes of this reform have been remarkably consistent over the years. In his book on 19th century reform, *The Irony of Early School Reform*, University of Pennsylvania sociologist Michael Katz, found these reformers were mainly upper-middle-class whites who controlled legislative and commercial interests, who had limited or no expertise in education, and who sought to provide a public education system that promulgated their particular idea of a well-ordered society. Katz found these reformers were remarkably paternalistic in their approach to schools and schooling, seeking to shape the working class into compliant contributors to their commercial ambitions.[2]

The reform efforts we are experiencing today have their roots in a 1983 report called, *A Nation at Risk*.[3] The report said that lax standards and a "tide of mediocrity" were threatening the nation's standing in the world. Because the report fit neatly into President Ronald Reagan's education agenda, *A Nation at Risk* became the platform for all educational reforms moving forward. It didn't matter that eight years later another government report found that on "nearly every measure" *A Nation at Risk* got it wrong. Instead of a steady decline, this so-called *Sandia Report*,[4] [5] found that scores on a variety of measures were actually showing a steady improvement. The *Sandia Report* was never released and by the time it was published in an obscure educational journal the narrative of failing schools had taken hold and federal and state educational policies were driven by his narrative.[6]

What is the recent history of education reform?

The current reform movement really gained steam in 2002 with the passage of the No Child Left Behind (NCLB) legislation during the George W. Bush administration. Decrying the "soft bigotry of low expectations", President Bush promoted the NCLB as a civil rights issue. This legislation, modeled after the practices Bush had instituted in Texas, sought to narrow the "achievement gap" between affluent, mostly white, suburban students and poor, mostly minority, urban students. The narrowing of this "achievement gap" was to be accomplished mainly by instituting yearly tests, closely monitoring the performance of sub-groups like minorities, English language learners and special education students and setting a goal of 100% student proficiency by 2014. The goal of meeting all students' needs was a laudable one, of course, but the law set goals that were clearly unattainable and sought to achieve these unattainable goals through testing children and punishing schools and teachers.

By setting impossible to meet target goals and by then labeling schools and teachers as "failing" if they could not meet those goals, NCLB contributed mightily to the impression that our schools were not performing well, our teachers were not doing their jobs, and the nation was at risk of falling behind other countries as leaders in the worlds of business, economics and technology. The impact on schools and teachers was devastating. Faced with impossible goals and public ridicule, teacher morale suffered mightily.

As the public began to buy into the narrative of failing public schools, reformers found an audience willing to consider laws that allowed the diversion of monies meant to support public schools to publicly funded but privately run charter schools, and school vouchers that would give parents a check to send their children where they wished. Arguing that all parents deserved a "choice" in schooling for their children, just as wealthy parents had the choice of a private school; reformers, funded by wealthy plutocrats who saw a ripe market to exploit, got charter school legislation passed in most states. The period saw unprecedented growth in these public charters, especially in urban areas, where many, many schools were labeled as "failing."

Another result of NCLB was that states, unable to meet the impossible learning targets, began to game the tests by lowering standards or commissioning tests that allowed them to show progress. A group of education reformers, funded by billionaire technology guru and philanthropist Bill Gates, determined that what we needed were national standards. Thus was born the Common Core State Standards. These standards, which are explained in detail in Chapter 8, were designed to ensure that all children from Mississippi to Minnesota and New Jersey to California were aiming at the same targets.

By the time President Barack Obama took office it was clear that NCLB was a failure. Instead of scrapping the entire "test and punish" platform that was NCLB, Obama, through his education secretary, the reform minded Arne Duncan, decided to double down on NCLB and so Race to the Top (RTTP) was born. The administration offered states stimulus monies to adopt the Common Core (or like standards), to continue yearly testing, and to evaluate teachers based on student test scores. If the states agreed, they not only got the money, but were allowed a waiver to get out from under the impossible to meet NCLB requirements, which, through legislative inertia, remained the law of the land. States, strapped for cash after the Great Recession of 2008, willingly signed on to the scheme.

At this writing the reform agenda continues to dominate the world of public education. Describing their mission as the "civil rights issue of our time", reformers, backed by billionaire plutocrats, continue to push for more testing, more labeling of schools, more teacher accountability and more school choice. Unsurprisingly, these reformers are very much like the education reformers of 150 years ago: rich, powerful, and paternalistic; lacking educational experience and knowledge of practice; and determined to have a public education system that creates compliant citizens and workers.

Who are today's education reformers?

As in the past, education reform today is driven largely from outside the educational establishment. Reformers see this as a good thing, since their view is that professional educators are part of the problem and too invested in the status quo to lead the changes that the reformers see as necessary. A few of these reformers have less than altruistic motives for their entry into education reform. Some conservative corporate types see reform as a vehicle for attacking unions, in this case the teacher unions, or for driving home a world view that competition is good in all things.

Other education reformers see the huge taxpayer funded public school system as a good investment opportunity, and go into education reform to push for policies that will allow for the privatization of public schools and the huge profits that may follow. Most education reformers are, however, well-meaning. They see a problem, low international test scores, struggling inner-city schools, and they want to do something to fix it. This is admirable, but may be problematic if they don't actually understand the problem or how to fix it.

Education reformers can be divided into three main camps: wealthy philanthropists looking to spend their charitable dollars well (and just possibly profiting from their own charity), non-profit organizations and their leaders, and politicians. Their efforts, and their funding, are all intertwined and inter-connected.

Wealthy Philanthropists

Bill Gates, the founder and former CEO of Microsoft, retired from his company to devote his time to the Bill and Melinda Gates Foundation, a philanthropic organization that has increasingly turned its attention to public education. In the early 2000s, Gates funded a "small schools initiative" intended to improve education in the inner city by breaking large high schools into smaller more manageable schools that would combine "rigor and relationships" to improve student achievement. By 2006, Gates had abandoned the idea because the results were not encouraging.[7]

In more recent years Gates has spent millions on two of the centerpieces of education reform: The Common Core State Standards (CCSS) and teacher evaluation based on test scores. Gates has given millions of dollars to develop and promote the CCSS, both through direct monetary support and through grants to other groups who push for the adoption and implementation of the CCSS.[8] Gates also funded the largest ever study of teacher effectiveness, called The Measures of Effective Teaching, with the stated aim of improving the way that teachers are evaluated and improving the feedback they get from such evaluations. Both the Common Core and teacher evaluation will be looked at in detail in later chapters. For now we can say that there can be little question that many of the key tenets of education reform are being driven by Gates Foundation money.

The Walton family, of Walmart and Sam's Club fame, direct their philanthropy through The Walton Family Foundation. Coming from the world of cutthroat retail competition, and, some would say, unfair labor and business tactics, the Walton's look to use their money to push their world view on public education. Their vision for public schools is one that:

> *... infuse[s] competitive pressure into the nation's K-12 education system by increasing the quantity and quality of school choices available to parents, especially in low-income communities.*[9]

With this philosophy it is not surprising that the Walton's are funding charter schools and voucher efforts across the country.

Eli Broad, a wildly successful business man, founder of two Fortune 500 companies, invests his money in education reform through The Eli and Edythe Broad Foundation. Broad's big idea is to improve schools through training school leaders to run school districts the way Broad ran his businesses. Broad established the Broad Superintendents Academy to train such leaders. These leaders are trained in management and finance and encouraged to use such strategies as closing struggling schools and opening more charter schools as a way to improve school performance. Broad Superintendent Academy graduates have proven to be highly controversial and of questionable effectiveness, perhaps in part because so many had little education background prior to their Broad training.[10]

Non-Profit Organizations

Non-profits are organizations that spend whatever revenue they might generate to further their purpose or mission, rather than claiming private profit or paying dividends to stockholders as for-profits do. Non-profits in the education reform arena are often heavily subsidized by the wealthy philanthropists, who look for these groups to further their education reform agendas. Among the most important non-profits in education reform are the Thomas B. Fordham Institute, Teach for America, Students First, and Democrats for Education Reform.

The Thomas B. Fordham Institute is an ideologically conservative think tank that receives much of its funding from the Gates Foundation. Leadership of the group includes former George W. Bush Secretary of Education, Rod Paige, and former Reagan Assistant Secretary of Education, Chester Finn. The Fordham Institute advocates for a wide range of education reforms and has been particularly focused on the implementation of the Common Core State Standards throughout the country.

Teach for America (TFA), founded by Wendy Kopp while she was a student at Princeton University, had as its original mission recruiting top performing students from elite universities to fill vacant teaching positions in inner city school districts desperate for teachers. From this one laudable idea, TFA has become a leading voice in the education reform movement and has attracted donations, including 5 million from the Walton Family Foundation and a 50-million-dollar grant from the U. S. Department of Education, to grow and expand its mission. Education reform critics like Gary Rubinstein, a former TFA teacher, and former Fordham board member Diane Ravitch, now view TFA as an ideologically driven organization that is delivering inadequately trained teachers, undermining teacher unions, displacing certified career teachers in many cities, and contributing to the spread of charter schools.[11]

Students First is an education reform movement founded by Michelle Rhee after she left her position as chancellor of the Washington, DC school district, a position she took after having been a TFA teacher for three years in Baltimore, MD and then founding a reform minded organization, The New Teacher Project. Rhee is perhaps the best known and certainly most controversial of all the education reformers. Students First is the vehicle for driving her agenda. In their 2013 "policy report card", Students First called for ending teacher tenure and seniority protections, merit pay for teachers based on student scores on standardized tests, and removing any caps on class size.[12]

Democrats for Education Reform (DFER) is a New York City based political action committee dedicated to getting Democrats to embrace education reform. The group has received millions of dollars in donations from the Walton Family Foundation and from media mogul and Fox News owner, Rupert Murdoch. As Diane Ravitch has noted, the DFER is also heavily supported by wealthy Wall Street hedge fund managers. The DFER spends heavily in state and local elections to support candidates favorable to charter schools and evaluating teachers using test scores.[13] The DFER has also participated in referenda to undermine teacher job protections in California and in advertising to encourage attacks on the teacher union in Chicago.

Politicians

As noted above, the recent history of education reform can be traced directly to President George W. Bush through No Child Left Behind and President Barack Obama through Race to the Top. Obama's Secretary of Education Arne Duncan has been a particularly vocal advocate for the Common Core, for standardized testing, and for evaluating teachers based on student test scores. Former Florida Governor and George's brother, Jeb Bush, led extensive education reform movements in Florida that saw a huge increase in the number of charter schools and the expansion of standardized testing with very mixed results. Jeb Bush parlayed his reformer credentials into an education reform think tank, The Chiefs for Change, a group that has been working to push a reform agenda across the country.

Several state governors, both Republican and Democrat, have championed educational reform including most notably Mario Cuomo in New York, Scott Walker in Milwaukee, Chris Christie in New Jersey and Mitch Daniels in Indiana. These state reform efforts have often been tied to teacher job protections, expansion of school choice, and reduction of collective bargaining rights for teachers. Bush, Walker and Christie have tried to parlay their tough stance on teacher unions onto the national stage as presidential candidates.

Current Senator and former Mayor of Newark, New Jersey, Cory Booker, is a champion of education reform. He rather famously brokered the deal that brought a 100-million-dollar donation to the Newark schools from Facebook founder, Mark Zuckerberg. A recent book by journalist Dale Russakoff, *The Prize*, chronicles how that 100 million has essentially disappeared without any appreciable improvement in the plight of Newark's school children, chiefly because the problems facing any large urban school district were misunderstood, the community was excluded from the decision making, and the proposed solutions were inadequate to deal with the complexity of the problems.[14]

Whether they mean well or not, the legacy of the education reformers is mixed at best. Much of the problem stems from the reformers being outsiders in the very complex arena of public education. If reformers hope to make more real progress for children in the future they may find that they need to address the underlying problems that lead to educational underachievement, chiefly poverty and health care, and they may also need to team up with the local parents, students, teachers and educational leaders who are the key stakeholders in this enterprise.

What issues motivate education reformers?

The main motivation for education reformers is their view that public education in America is mediocre at best and abysmal at worst, particularly in the large, poverty riddled cities in the country, and that this puts the country at a competitive disadvantage in the global marketplace. This view, which on cursory examination contains at least an element of truth, has been seized upon by many well-meaning reformers and philanthropists as an issue of social justice and equity. Most unfortunately, it has also been seized upon by an element in our society that sees public education both as a potential profit center and an opportunity to advance a social agenda that favors the "business model" of competition and disruption, and which distrusts all government led social programs.

These motivations have led to the corporate education reformers call for a variety of interventions designed to improve the quality of public education. These programs have centered on standardized testing and holding schools, teachers and children accountable based on these tests, school choice in the form of charter schools and vouchers, and stripping teacher unions of power and teachers of job protections like tenure. Each of these interventions and the consequences of these reforms will be discussed in subsequent chapters.

There can be no doubting that many of these education reformers are sincere, dedicated individuals who would like to improve the educational prospects of American schoolchildren. There can also be no doubt that all of these efforts will fail if the number one cause for the struggles of public education, and for that matter American society, is not addressed at the same time. Of course that cause is poverty.

When poverty is controlled for, the US stands at or near the top of performance on international tests of educational performance like the Program for International Assessment (PISA). So while teachers are the number one influence on a child's learning in school, out of school influences including familial, financial and environmental influences have a far greater impact.

Corporate education reformers tend to ignore poverty as a cause for low educational performance. Like many Americans they are enamored with the great American Horatio Alger myth that any child can succeed in America through hard work and a good education. It is the embracing of this myth that both resonates with so many people fighting for reform and which will be the ultimate Achilles heel of these reformers. While it is nice to believe as the reformers like to say that "poverty is not destiny", for the vast majority of the millions of children born into poverty in this country, poverty most certainly is destiny. Education is not a cure for poverty. In fact, poverty directly interferes with the ability to get a good education and reap the benefits of education.

What is the "achievement gap?"

The term **achievement gap** refers to the disparity in test scores between different groups of students, typically between white students and minority students. The achievement gap has proven to be very difficult to narrow. While No Child Left Behind was specifically designed to address the achievement gap, no appreciable narrowing of that gap has been accomplished. This is very likely because the achievement gap, which is a measure of educational outputs, is closely linked to an **opportunity gap**, the inequitable distribution of resources and opportunities that result from poverty and inadequate financial support of urban schools.

No Child Left Behind and its sequel Race to the Top have failed to address the opportunity gap in any meaningful way and so the achievement gap persists. No amount of test based accountability, attacks on teachers and teacher unions, or school choice schemes will narrow the gap, because none of these efforts address the underlying causes of that gap – poverty and the opportunity gap that accompanies poverty.

There is another aspect of the achievement gap that should be addressed here. Many students, especially those who enter school from impoverished households and neighborhoods, are perceived to have learning deficits. A **deficit model** of education consigns children to a lower rung on the achievement ladder before schooling even begins. This deficit model is driven by narratives about lack of vocabulary, lack of literacy materials in the home, and lack of parental engagement in the child's development. It is further entrenched in education by a slavish reliance on standardized test scores to measure knowledge and understanding.

Instead of a deficit model, educators would do well to embrace a **difference model;** a model that acknowledges and celebrates the different ways that students come to learning. A model that recognizes that every child presents a profile of learning strengths, learning needs and individual interests may help us move on from a narrative about **achievement gaps** to one of **achievement opportunities.**

What parents should ask from any school their child attends are these very tangible, very individual **achievement opportunities.**

What is a "failing" school?

The No Child Left Behind (NCLB) act brought the term "low performing school" into the vocabulary of education reform. The press and the public shortened the terminology adopting a term familiar to all who have attended school: "failing." And thus the term "failing school" was born. By NCLB definition a failing school was one that failed to meet "adequate yearly progress" (AYP) on student standardized test achievement measures for various student sub-groups two years in a row. As mentioned previously, NCLB put up progress benchmarks that were impossible to meet, so many schools, including affluent schools, but especially schools in poor, urban areas, were found to be failing.

NCLB provided that schools found to be "failing" were required to take a variety of steps to improve performance up to and including replacing the entire teaching staff, closing the school or turning the school into a charter school. For many urban schools, faced with goals that could not be met and threatened with closure and takeover by charter schools, the impact on the morale of the administrators, teaching staff, parents and children was devastating.

These schools, teachers and families were being asked to accept the label of failure, when in reality they had been failed by an inequitable, unjust system. Ultimately, NCLB and the entire narrative of "failing schools" resulted in punishing and blaming rather than improving education. This blame game resulted in the proliferation of charter schools, school voucher programs and other measures that accelerated the already precipitous decline of public education in American cities like New Orleans, Philadelphia, and Chicago. All of this was done without any appreciable improvement in overall student performance or any narrowing of the achievement gap.

Are the problems in public education cited by education reformers real?

Yes, American public education has many problems. Most of these problems can be laid at the feet of more general societal problems like poverty, inequity and de facto segregation. There are other school-based problems, however, that are real and need to be addressed. Here is a list of these problems. These issues are not new for the most part and professional educators are well aware of them, but solutions have been elusive. Each of the problems here is a generalization; exemplary programs exist across the country that deal well with these issues, but the problems persist.

1. **Schools that are clean, safe and adequately resourced** – If you use public transportation, drive on public highways or visit many urban school buildings, you know that America has allowed its infrastructure to fall into disrepair through neglect and failure to spend the money necessary. Every child deserves a safe, clean place to learn that is adequately stocked with the tools of learning – books, paper, pencils, technology, science laboratories, visual and performing arts spaces, gymnasiums and athletic fields. Our failure to garner sufficient tax revenues to ensure that all students can go to schools like this is a national disgrace.

2. **Meeting individual student needs** – Public schools are not very good at responding to individual student differences. Schools are institutions and like all institutions, they struggle to accommodate individual differences. Smaller class sizes (which cost money) better teacher professional development in differentiating instruction, and improved parent/school communication, are some ways to deal with this issue.

3. **Graduates who are prepared to do well in college** – If a child chooses to go to college, the public schools should provide curriculum and instruction that prepare the student for that choice. The proliferation of remedial courses

at the college level is pointed to as evidence that many high school graduates are not well-prepared. This is the issue that the Common Core State Standards is supposed to address. In my experience the curriculum to prepare a child for college is in place in nearly all schools and was long before the Common Core was a gleam in Bill Gates' eye. What is often not in place is a level of communication between school, child and parent that helps parents and students know where they are on the way to college preparedness and what all players can do to ensure preparedness.

4. **Teacher evaluation** – Again, while exemplary practices in evaluating teachers exist, they are the exception and not the rule. In many cases this is the result of understaffing in schools, but it is also the result of failure to make evaluation a priority. Education reformers tend to focus on evaluation that will identify poorly performing teachers and test-based accountability for performance, while a wiser approach would be one that focuses on teacher improvement and retention.

5. **Teacher quality** – Every child deserves a well-qualified, well-educated, caring professional teacher in every classroom. Not every child is getting one. As is true in all professions, the teaching profession has some high performers, some average performers and some poor performers. To ensure that every child gets the best teachers possible we must see that highly motivated individuals enter the profession, that teacher preparation programs in colleges and universities are producing highly prepared educators, and that new teachers get the support they need in the school buildings. We also need to ensure that high quality teachers are choosing to work in areas of great need.

While these problems are real, there is no evidence that the education reform agenda of national standards, test-based accountability, and school choice are the solutions. In fact, in most cases these approaches only exacerbate the problems. We will discuss these issues in detail in later chapters.

How will education reform impact public education?

The education reform agenda has the potential to destroy public education. In fact that may be the goal of reformers, who would prefer a business model of privatized education. As can already be seen in cities like New Orleans, Philadelphia, Chicago, Milwaukee and others, school choice in the form of charter schools and vouchers leeches money away from already cash strapped public schools, and further erodes the services schools can provide. Test-based accountability causes already admittedly struggling schools to focus on test scores rather than on rich curriculum, and the narrative that our schools are failing us and our teachers are failing our children undermines educator morale and makes education an unattractive career choice for prospective teachers.

Each of these issues will be dealt with in more detail as we take a closer look at testing, school choice, and teacher quality moving forward in the book.

How will education reform impact my child?

The impact of education reform on the individual child is not yet clear. Much of the impact will depend on where you live, with urban children likely to feel the greatest impact.

We know that a heavy emphasis on test-based accountability

leads to more testing and more teaching to the test. With more testing and more test preparation comes limits on other school experiences like music, art and physical education; subjects that are not tested, but are very important to the broad education most parents want for their children. Test based accountability also tends to sort children into winners (high scorers) and losers (low scorers) with the resultant feelings of inadequacy that can come from not doing well.

Rigid adherence to educational standards that may not be developmentally appropriate could also have an impact on your child. Young children, especially, show a wide range of readiness for formal instruction. Teachers need the latitude and autonomy to make professional judgments about what instruction is best for a particular child. Standards, tied to standardized tests, may inhibit teachers' ability to make these decisions for the child.

School choice can also be disruptive for children. School choice programs like those in Newark, NJ have resulted in children traveling all over the city to attend a school, rather than attending a local neighborhood school. Other students have been forced to change schools in the middle of the year as charter schools shut their doors. Still others have "chosen" online charter schools which have shown very poor learning results.

What resources will help me learn more about education reform?

For book length rationales of education reform in general try these:

Hanushek, E., Peterson, P. and Woessmann, L. (2013). *Endangering Prosperity: A Global View of the American School.* NY: Brooking Institution Press.

Finn, C. and Sousa, R. (2014). *What Lies Ahead for America's Children and Their Schools.* NY: Hoover Institution Press.

Petrilli, M. (2012). *The Diverse Schools Dilemma: A Parent's Guide to Sociologically Mixed Urban Schools.* NY: Thomas B. Fordham Institute.

Smarick, A. (2012). *The Urban School System of the Future: Applying the Principles and Lessons of Chartering.* NY: Rowman and Littlefield Education.

For book length critiques of the education reform movement try these:

Cody, A. (2014). *The Educator and the Oligarch.* NY: Garn Press.

Ravitch, D. (2013). *Reign of Error: The Hoax of the Privatization Movement and the Threat to America's Public Schools.* NY: Knopf.

Ravitch, D. (2010). *The Death and Life of the Great American School System: How Testing and Choice are Undermining Education.* NY: Knopf.

Berliner, D.C. and Glass, G.V. (2014). *50 Myths and Lies that Threaten America's Public Schools: The Real Crisis in Education.* NY: Teachers College Press.

Schneider, M.K. (2014). *A Chronicle of Echoes.* Charlotte, NC: Information Age Publishing.

Kuhn, J. (2014). *Fear and Learning in America.* NY: Teachers College Press.

Lubienski, C. and Lubienski, S. (2013). *The Public School Advantage: Why Public Schools Outperform Private Schools.* Chicago: University of Chicago Press.

For articles that support the educational reform movement try these:

Bireda, S. (March, 23, 2010). A Primer on the New Elementary and Secondary Education Act. *Center for American Progress.* https://www.americanprogress.org/issues/education/

report/2010/03/23/7465/education-reform-101/

R. M. (April 1, 2010). Eight Questions for Chester Finn. *The Economist.* http://www.economist.com/blogs/lexington/2010/04/education_reform

For an article length critique of education reform try this:

Strauss, V. (October 26, 2010). A Primer on Corporate School Reform. *The Washington Post.* http://www.washingtonpost.com/blogs/answer-sheet/post/a-primer-on-corporate-school-reform/2011/10/26/gIQAyWrUKM_blog.html

2

The Qualities of a Good School

What are the key characteristics of a good school?

All parents want to send their children to a "good" school. But what is it that makes a school a good school? Are good schools those that achieve high standardized test scores as No Child Left Behind, Race to the Top and education reformers would have us believe? Or is a good school more than that? Is it possible that a school with mediocre or even low test scores is still a good school?

You can find many books and articles on what makes a good school. I have listed a number of them at the end of this chapter. All these ideas can be boiled down to a few basic concepts. Good schools are those that provide for: [15]

- A clean, safe, well-organized and caring learning environment.
- Strong, highly professional, highly-collaborative administration and teaching staff.

- A broad educational program available to all students.
- A belief system that says all children can learn if taught well, coupled with high expectations for learning.
- An ongoing and varied assessment system that informs teachers and leads to good instruction.
- A high level of community involvement and support.

A new organization, *Schools of Opportunity,* does the best job I have seen in putting these basic precepts into context and defining what makes a good school, not based on test scores, but on the opportunities for learning that the school provides for children. *Schools for Opportunity* grew from the concern of the organizers that typical awards for schools tended to favor schools that enroll students who have the richest learning opportunities outside of school. In other words recognition as an exemplary school went to schools in affluent areas. The organizers, including award winning principal, Carol Burris and Director of the National Education Policy Center, Kevin Welner, sought a better way to assess quality and reward excellence, and thus the *Schools of Opportunity* recognition program was born.

Of most interest for us in defining quality schools are the criteria that *Schools of Opportunity* uses to determine what schools provide the best chance for students to learn and achieve. Basing their list of qualities on research and years of experience in teaching and leadership, *Schools of Opportunity* looked for schools to develop programs which: [16]

- **Create and maintain a healthy school culture** – This is, of course, similar to what is stated above, but *Schools of Opportunity* also focuses on effective practices to deal with bullying, harassment and discrimination that interfere with learning. The role of parents and the community in helping to foster a healthy school culture is also part of the criteria.

- **Broaden and enrich school curriculum** – Does the school provide a broad educational program that includes not only the core subjects of language arts, math, science and social studies, but also the visual and performing arts and physical education?

- **Provide more and better learning time during and after the school year** – A critical aspect of a school of opportunity is providing learning activities before and after school and during the summer. This is particularly important for disadvantaged students who may not have such learning opportunities outside of the school.

- **End disparities in learning opportunities reinforced by tracking** – Tracking is a system of channeling students into certain courses based on a perception of academic ability. Schools that track students deny learning opportunities to many. Part of fostering a school built on high-expectations for learning is providing all students with opportunities to take Advanced Placement, International Baccalaureate and other college preparatory courses.

- **Use a variety of assessments designed to respond to student needs** – Testing is best used as a way to inform teachers about how well students are learning and about instructional and curricular revisions that may be necessary. Schools of opportunity use authentic assessments at the center of the program and de-emphasize the use of standardized tests in evaluating students.

- **Reassess student discipline policies** – In order to reap the benefits of schooling, students need to be in school. School discipline practices that focus on exclusion from class through in or out of school suspension often disproportionately impact students of color. Schools of opportunity are constantly reassessing their discipline policies to be sure they are not denying children learning opportunities.

- **Support teachers as professionals** – A good school has a strong mentoring program for new teachers that links the neophyte to an experienced master teacher. A good school is one where teachers are given the time and the support needed to collaborate with each other on curriculum, instruction and assessment. A good school provides ample on-going professional development for teachers to hone their skills.

- **Provide adequate resources to support a well-maintained school environment** – Dirty, dilapidated, ill-repaired school buildings are a national disgrace and work against student learning. Parents and community members need to insist on school buildings that can be pointed to with pride.

- **Address key health issues** – Good health is a pre-requisite for good learning. A school of opportunity provides for this through a professionally staffed health office and screening programs for hearing, vision, nutrition and dental care.

- **Build on the strengths of language minority students** – Schools of opportunity view their language minority students as assets and approach the learning of English in a way that respects the child's first language and encourages bilingualism. Good schools embrace the diversity that different language cultures bring to the school.

- **Expand access to libraries and the internet** – Good schools have well-maintained, well- stocked, professionally managed libraries. Good schools also provide access to technology to all students and ensure that the technology is used appropriately as a tool for learners and teachers and not a replacement for instruction.

In assessing the quality of the school where they will send their children, parents should consider the quality of the opportunities that the school provides for all students.

What do standardized tests tell me about school quality?

Standardized tests are best at showing overall trends and possible areas of concern. They can, therefore be useful as part of a broad look at school quality. The important thing to remember is that standardized tests scores are only one small part of the overall picture. UCLA professor, W. James Popham says flatly that standardized tests should not be used to measure the quality of schools because the tests are designed to detect differences in learning in individual students. Since students in different schools come from different levels of advantage and disadvantage, standardized test scores cannot be used to evaluate school quality.[17]

Whenever standardized test scores are used in comparisons of school quality, two questions must be asked:

1. Do these schools serve the same number of disadvantaged, special needs and second language learners?
2. Were those test scores achieved through a quality program that offers broad opportunities to all children or through a single minded focus on raising the test scores?

Look at test scores skeptically and weigh what the test scores tell you about the other things you see at the school that are indicators of quality. Most importantly, is your child engaged, happy and learning based on multiple measures including teacher reports and your own observations? You can read more on standardized testing in Chapter 9.

What constitutes a rich school program of learning?

Good schools offer children lots of opportunities for learning in a broad array of subjects. Emphasis in elementary schools should be on developing literacy (reading, writing, speaking, listening) skills and mathematical (computation and conceptual) skills. Large blocks of time, two hours daily for reading and writing and one hour daily for mathematics are ideal. Elementary schools should also offer a firm grounding in social studies (history, government, sociology, psychology) and the sciences (life, earth, chemical, physical). Strong programs in the visual and performing arts including music appreciation, musical performance, art appreciation and drawing and painting should also be offered. Regularly scheduled physical education and health classes, as well as time for recess, should also be a part of a comprehensive elementary curriculum. Elementary schools should also provide after school opportunities in the form of clubs (chess, computers, library, chorus, intramural sports) that allow students to explore interests beyond the regular academic program.

Instruction in elementary schools should take place, for the most part, in a self-contained classroom. One of the major goals of the elementary program is that teachers get to know their students very well and that these young students have a "safe haven" of a classroom environment that is familiar and comfortable. Currently many schools are adopting a "platooning" model for elementary students where students change classes based on the subjects being taught, perhaps having one teacher for language arts and another for math and science. The argument is that teachers will be able to "specialize" in the content they teach.[18] The research is inconclusive on the academic benefit of such models, but the social and emotional costs to young children should be clear. Elementary teachers are whole-child oriented rather than specific content oriented. In other words, they teach children, not subjects. The current obsession with test scores is driving the efforts to compartmentalize elementary education. The social and emotional costs to children of this departmental structure could be great. As the University of New Hampshire's Joe Onosko, Paula Salvio and Clio Stearns put it:

> *Sadly, when school success is reduced to achievement gains on standardized tests in two subject areas, and teacher time with each child is reduced to less than an hour each day, the potential for a child to develop an emotional attachment to a caring adult, one who is deeply knowledgeable about and dedicated to their full development, is lost.*[19]

Middle school (grades 6-8 and sometimes 5-8) is an appropriate time to introduce departmentalization. The combination of student maturity and increased content demands make specialization desirable at this age. Students again should be taking courses in all the core subjects with, ideally, at least 90 minutes for the language arts and 45 minutes for other subjects. Art, music and physical education should again be a part of any middle school program.

Middle schools should also expand students' opportunities for choice as they begin to look forward to more specialized study. These programs should include a choice of world languages, as well as specializations in art, theater, and music, including chorus, band and orchestra, computing, and others. After school programs should expand to include a wide variety of clubs, including literary, computer based and mathematics clubs, and both intra- and inter-mural sports.

At the high school level, the increasing maturity of the students and the preparation for life after high school make a rich and varied program with a great deal of student choice ideal. Besides the core courses discussed above, high schools should offer all students opportunities for advanced study in Advanced Placement and/ or International Baccalaureate courses. Entry into these courses should not be restricted, but open to all who are interested and willing to do the work required.

High schools should also offer programs for students who wish to pursue careers in a variety of trades from plumbing to computer programming. Wide choice and an opportunity for exploration are the keys to a good program. Again a wide variety of after school clubs, activities and sports are required to help students explore their many interests. Many high school students have found their career paths through high school service learning programs, where students do internships working with young children, children with disabilities, nursing home patients, etc. Programs like these help students explore career options, while also developing a sense of social responsibility.

What should be the targeted class sizes for a school?

Class size matters. Class size matters because it is an issue that impacts the lives of the children in the classroom, the work load of the teacher, and the school budget. Teachers and their representatives argue for smaller class sizes, while school boards try to balance parent and teacher desires for small classes, with the demands of keeping the budget under control. Apparently, private schools think class size matters. They advertise small class size in an effort to attract students to their schools.

Intuitively, most parents and teachers think class size matters, but from a research standpoint the impact of class size has been harder to pin down. At the heart of the argument is the question, "Do the academic gains achieved through smaller class sizes justify the cost of hiring more teachers to accommodate those lower class sizes?" Some education reformers have even suggested that children would be better off if schools would identify their best teachers and then pay those teachers a premium to accept more students in their classes.[20]

A research study done in Tennessee is considered the gold standard of class size studies because of its rigorous experimental design. This so-called STAR study[21] found that students in small classes learned more than students in larger classes and were more likely to complete school and attend college, but those small classes were so small that the STAR study simply rekindled the cost/benefit debate.

More recently, Northwestern University professor Diane Whitmore Schanzenbach published a study through the National Education Policy Center that summarized what we know about class size. Considering all the research as a whole she concluded that: [22]

- *Class size is an important determinant of student outcomes, and one that can be directly determined by policy.*
- *The evidence suggests that increasing class size will harm not only children's test scores in the short run, but also their long-run human capital formation. Money saved today by increasing class sizes will result in more substantial social and educational costs in the future.*
- *The payoff from class-size reduction is greater for low-income*

and minority children, while any increases in class size will likely be most harmful to these populations.

- *Policymakers should carefully weigh the efficacy of class-size policy against other potential uses of funds. While lower class size has a demonstrable cost, it may prove the more cost-effective policy overall.*

So class size does matter, it matters especially for low-income and minority children, and it is likely to be worth the taxpayers' money to attempt to keep class sizes down.

Research does not help us much with what the ideal class sizes should be. The STAR study targeted class sizes of 13-17 children, which may be out of the financial reach of many districts. As a school district administrator several years ago, I was tasked with developing target ranges for class sizes for a suburban school district. After reading the available research and consulting with the budget office, I came up with the following recommendations. As parents, I would recommend that you look at these recommendations as broad guidelines and not set in stone. A variation of a student or two from these numbers does not mean that students are necessarily being disadvantaged, but large deviations may be of concern.

Recommended Class Sizes by Grade Range

K-2	20-22
3-8	23-25
9-12	23-27

Courses designed for students with special needs or for students who need focused instruction on certain skills should be smaller, normally about 8-12 students. Also, these class size recommendations were developed for a relatively affluent community; smaller class sizes would likely be necessary to successfully serve students in low-income neighborhoods.

What is the role of the principal in a quality school?

Research cited by Leadership Matters indicates that the school principal is second only to classroom instruction in impacting the quality of student learning.[23] According to the Mid-Continent Research for Education and Learning (McREL):

> *Effective school leaders know how to focus the work of the school on the essential. They have a clear mission or purpose for the school and identify goals that align with that mission. They communicate the purpose and goals in a meaningful way such that all stakeholders understand what they need to do.*[24]

Leadership Matters goes on to say that school leaders impact student learning in the following ways:[25]

- By shaping a vision of academic success for all students.
- By fostering a climate of collaboration that is conducive to learning.
- By cultivating leadership in others so that teachers and other adults in the school help to shape the school's vision.
- By working with teachers to improve instruction for all students.
- By managing people, data and processes to foster school improvement.

To this list I would add crucially:

- By communicating clearly with the entire school community about the school's vision and educational program.

Obviously, a school principal has a complex job demanding great skill and with many demands on time. Parents should expect an instructional leader who has a deep understanding of quality instruction, a good relationship with the teachers, is well-known to the students, and communicates clearly, informatively and frequently with parents.

What learning supports should be available for my child?

A good school provides students with the learning supports they need to be successful. Not all students learn at the same pace and under the same learning conditions. Some students need more time to learn certain skills, while others may need alternate forms of instruction or more intensive instruction to learn. Schools need to have a professional staff ready and able to identify student learning difficulties and to provide the needed interventions.

At a minimum a school should have access to a school psychologist, a learning disabilities specialist and a school social worker. Smaller schools may share these professionals with other schools and in some cases these services may be provided by a county or state agency. These three people typically work as a team, sometimes called a Child Study Team, to consult with teachers and parents about all aspects of an individual child's intellectual, behavioral, social and emotional experience in school. The school psychologist may counsel individual students and their families and provide testing to determine student learning potential and needs. The learning disabilities consultant works with teachers and parents to recommend specific instructional interventions that a student might need. The school social worker works with the family and the student to resolve social and emotional issues in school.

The work of the Child Study Team is supported by a team of teachers, often with the special training needed to work with students with learning differences. Good schools employ speech therapists, reading specialists, English as a second language teachers, occupational therapists, and teachers trained and certificated in special education to meet the needs of these students. Students might receive services in the regular classroom, where the specialist comes into the room and works with the teacher to provide needed learning interventions, or in small group "pull-out" sessions where the student can get the needed instruction outside the regular classroom.

Determining if your child needs any of these services can be fraught with emotion for both you as the parent and for your child. Good schools follow a protocol for assistance that seeks to provide the interventions needed in collaboration with parents and with the least amount of disruption to the child as possible. Most schools use some variation of a protocol called Response to Intervention (RTI).[26] RTI has three tiers of support for a child. The purpose of RTI is to make sure all students get the support they need to learn with the least disruption to the regular school routine as possible. The process begins with a teacher or sometimes a parent who recognizes a learning difficulty and asks the child study team for assistance. In Tier 1, interventions take place in the regular classroom. The child study team, reading specialist or others might suggest ways that a teacher might modify or differentiate instruction to help the struggling learner. Tier 1 progress is monitored and after a period of time, perhaps 4-8 weeks, results of the Tier 1 intervention are reviewed.

If the Tier 1 intervention is proving successful, then these interventions are continued. If these interventions do not appear to be successful and improved learning is not evident, the student may be moved to a Tier 2 intervention. In a Tier 2 intervention, students are provided instruction in small groups two or three times a week, again either within the regular class or as a "pull-out." This instruction may be provided by a specialist, such as a reading specialist, English as a second language teacher, or a basic skills teacher. Again progress is monitored for a period of weeks and these interventions are either continued, determined to have been successful and discontinued, or moved on to Tier 3.

Tier 3 involves more intensive small group instruction, usually outside of the regular classroom and generally five days a week. If after a period of weeks, Tier 3 interventions are not found successful, the student will generally be referred for testing to see if special education services are required. This testing is often done by the school psychologist or the reading specialist. Results of the testing will be used to determine if a child needs specific special education services. These services generally require a teacher specially trained in working with children with learning disabilities. Even when a child is identified for special education services, much of the instruction the child receives will happen in the regular classroom, often by a team consisting of a regular education teacher and a special education teacher.

The purpose of all of these services is to provide struggling learners the help they need when they need it and in "the least restrictive environment (LRE)." LRE is a legal requirement from the U.S. Individuals with Disabilities Act that requires that children with disabilities be educated with non-disabled peers to the greatest extent possible.

As you investigate your local public school, or others schools you may be considering for your child, you may want to ask questions about the kinds of interventions they provide for struggling learners and what protocol they follow when deciding if children need these services.

What non-instructional staff should be available in my child's school?

A school is a small community. As such a school needs to provide a variety of services that a small community needs. Many of these needs are filled by non-instructional staff, people who work alongside the teachers and administrators to make sure that kids' needs are being met. When schools are in distressed communities, they may need more of these non-instructional staff to meet the needs of kids growing up in a neighborhood that does not provide traditional health and welfare supports. A good school has, at the very least, the following non-instructional staff: nurses, guidance counselors, librarians, custodians, teacher assistants, and bus drivers.

Healthy students learn better than unhealthy ones. School nurses provide vital vision and hearing screenings as well as assessments of students' general health, medication for students with allergies and other health concerns, first aid and emergency medical services. They are often on the frontline of noting family issues that may be impacting a student's health or ability to focus in class. The number of nurses a school needs varies with the level of wellness of the general school population. According to the National Association of School Nurses, schools with student populations with high health needs need one nurse for every 125 children, while schools with relatively well populations need one nurse for every 750 students.[27]

Guidance counselors provide vital services to children in all schools. Here is just a partial list of the many services guidance counselors perform:

- Individual student academic program planning.
- Interpreting cognitive, aptitude and achievement tests.
- Providing counseling to students who are tardy or absent.
- Providing counseling to students who have disciplinary problems.
- Providing counseling to students as to appropriate school dress.
- Providing college and career counseling.
- Collaborating with teachers to present school counseling core curriculum lessons.
- Analyzing grade-point averages in relationship to achievement.
- Interpreting student records.
- Providing teachers with suggestions for effective classroom management.
- Ensuring student records are maintained as per state and federal regulations.
- Helping the school principal identify and resolve student issues, needs and problems.
- Providing individual and small-group counseling services to students.
- Advocating for students at individual education plan meet-

ings, student study teams and school attendance review boards.

- Providing liaison services between students and college admissions offices.

The American School Counselor Association recommends a school counselor to student ratio of 1:250 and that school counselors spend 80 percent or more of their time in direct and indirect services to students.[28]

A school librarian is central to any successful school program. One of the most disheartening aspects of the recent belt tightening in school budgets is that many schools have eliminated librarians. I am tempted to say that the current trend to eliminating librarians in schools is a sure sign of the decline of western civilization. Perhaps that sounds a bit hyperbolic, but the truth is that a professionally certified school librarian is vital to the learning health of a school. One way to determine your school's commitment to all children learning is to check out the library and make sure that it is adequately staffed and the shelves are well stocked. We all know that librarians order books, assist children in finding books related to their interests, check out books and make sure books get returned. Here are some services school librarians provide that you may not be so aware of. Among many other things, school librarians:[29]

- Teach students how to locate, select, create and share information.

- Help students link online sources of information with print sources.

- Help students develop responsibility through returning materials and using online media appropriately.

- Assist teachers by identifying resources to supplement classroom instruction, developing subject specific bibliographies and ordering resources to support curriculum.

- Provide access to library resources beyond the school day.
- Manage a vast array of resources for students and teachers.
- Bring stories to children through book talks and read-alouds.
- Know about media and literature for children and young adults.
- Meet diverse student needs and interests.
- Challenge children to think critically about what they read or see.

Teacher assistants provide support for teachers in a variety of ways including assisting in managing the classroom and reinforcing classroom routines, reinforcing lessons provided by the teacher through review for those who need it, supervising students in class, hallways and lunch rooms, and assisting the teacher in preparing materials for instruction. Some teacher assistants are assigned as aides to an individual student who may need particular learning assistance. Obviously, these para-professionals play a large and important role in the school and are in constant contact with students. A good school will, therefore, have a rigorous hiring and training process to be sure that teacher assistants are skilled at working with and understanding children.

Dwindling school budgets and school district financial distress have led many schools to move toward privatizing school bus drivers and school custodians. It is often cheaper to hire an outside firm to manage the hiring and supervision for these school employees, because the private bus and custodial companies offer lower pay with fewer benefits and remove the cost of supervision from the district.

There are two reasons why I believe this is a short sighted cost cutting measure that does not serve the community, the parents, or the children well. The first reason is that people who fill positions as bus drivers and custodians generally live in the school district, pay taxes in the school district, and have both loyalty and a personal connection to the district. Private companies will be looking for the cheapest possible labor sources without regard to residence, so the employees do not have the same level of commitment to the schools, not to mention the tax revenues that are not coming to the district from these outside employees. The second reason is that when a school district is hiring and supervising bus drivers they have a better grasp on the quality of the individuals they are employing. Bus drivers and custodians interact with our children every day, and it is critical that they be good at interacting with children in ways that add to a child's school experience.

What is the role of the parent/teacher groups in a good school?

As we have seen above, good schools have effective community and parent involvement. One form that this involvement takes is through a parent organization, either a Parent Teacher Association (PTA) or Parent Teacher Organization (PTO). A school PTA is affiliated with the national PTA organization, follows the by-laws of the national organization, and pays dues to be a part of this group. A PTO is a local organization that is not affiliated with any national organization. The differences in how these groups function within any given school are minimal, but as part of a national organization PTAs do have a voice in national lobbying efforts on the part of parents of school aged children.

Whether PTA or PTO, parent organizations have an important role to play in the school. Active and well-organized parent organizations provide many services for the school. Perhaps the most visible of these services is fundraising. Parent organizations raise funds to provide the school with items that may be beyond the reach of the school budget. In the past, parent PTA/PTOs have provided for playground equipment, books for classroom libraries, technology infrastructure and general school supply needs. In the best case, PTA/PTOs work with the administration and teachers in a school to identify needs and set fundraising goals.

But parent organizations provide many other services to a school beyond financial support. Among these other services are the following.

- Encouraging parents to be involved in the life of the school.
- Assisting in fostering a healthy school culture.
- Scheduling special programs, forums and discussions for parents on topics of mutual interest and concern.
- Facilitating communication between parents and the school on key issues.
- Giving parents a voice in the operation of the school.

A vibrant, engaged parent organization is a vital part of a good school. All parents should make the effort to be a part of their school's parent organization.

What resources will help me learn more about quality schools?

For a description of the school recognition program *Schools of*

***Opportunity* go to their website:**

http://opportunitygap.org/

An older, but still useful description of quality schools written for parents by The Center for Research and Evaluation. Standard and Student Testing (CRESST) at UCLA can be found here:

CRESST. (1994). *A Guide to Parents and Communities Seeking Excellence in Education*. https://www.cse.ucla.edu/products/parents/cresst_GoodSchool.pdf

To get a sense of what high school students believe makes a quality school see this article:

Armstrong, S. (2002). What Makes a Good School: Students Speak Up at Leadership Forum. *Edutopia*. http://www.edutopia.org/what-makes-good-school-students-speak-leadership-forum

For a comprehensive report on charter school quality look here. The conclusions in the last few pages of this lengthy report from the Center for Research in Education Outcomes (CREDO) are particularly interesting:

Center for Research in Educational Outcomes. (2103). *National Charter School Study*. http://credo.stanford.edu/documents/NCSS%202013%20Final%20Draft.pdf

For a better understanding of the role of the principal in a quality school see this report:

National Association of Elementary School Principals. (2013). *What the Research Says about the Importance of Principal Leadership*. http://www.naesp.org/sites/default/files/LeadershipMatters.pdf

To learn more about parent teacher organizations look here:

http://www.pto.org/ and http://www.pta.org/

To learn more about Response to Intervention as a learning support program in the schools, see:

http://www.rtinetwork.org/learn/what/whatisrti

3

Readiness for School

What does "school readiness" mean?

If you google "readiness for school" or "readiness for kindergarten" or "readiness for first grade", you will find any number of checklists that purport to tell you if your child is "ready." In reality readiness is much more complicated than these checklists suggest. Readiness combines a number of factors. Here is how one group of early childhood researchers put it:

> *School readiness involves more than just children. School readiness, in the broadest sense, is about children, families, early environments, schools, and communities. Children are not innately "ready" or "not ready" for school. Their skills and development are strongly influenced by their families and through their interactions with other people and environments before coming to school.*[30]

It is not your child's job to be ready for school; it is the school's job to be ready for your child, and to meet your child's needs through rich curriculum, highly trained teachers and a system of learning supports. As the National Association of Elementary School Principals (NAESP) has said:

> *Schools should be ready for the child and not expect the child to be ready for the school. Early childhood programs must be based on the ways children learn, not on how adults prefer to teach.*[31]

Just as different children get teeth at different times and learn to walk at different times, young children will differ in their level of readiness for learning when they enter school. Parents, teachers and school district administrators must recognize this and must provide developmentally appropriate learning environments to meet these different children's differing needs. According to the NAEYC, Developmentally Appropriate Practice (DAP) means a learning framework designed to promote young children's optimal learning and development.[32]

What does a kindergarten that is ready for my child look like?

A kindergarten that is ready for children is one that recognizes that play is the work of childhood. Play in kindergarten is a special kind of play; it is play that is skillfully designed by the teacher to create environments for learning. According to researchers Bodrova and Leong, the kindergarten year:

> *... must emphasize the underlying skills that will make later academic success possible. This should be accomplished not by pushing down the curriculum goals and objectives of first grade, but by creating learning opportunities that will address the unique developmental accomplishments that ought to emerge in kindergarten.*[33]

What do children learn through structured play? The list of learning that takes place in appropriately structured block play and dramatic play is very long. Children learn to problem solve, sort and classify, work cooperatively, measure, balance, gain number sense, self-regulate, consider another's point of view, develop spatial awareness and delay gratification. Perhaps most impressively and importantly, children engaged in active and structured play with other children develop their oral language, their vocabulary, their ability to listen, sequence and retell, and their ability to represent objects and concepts symbolically. This oral language development becomes the child's greatest ally in coming to be literate.

But kindergarten should not be all play. There is plenty of room for academic content in the kindergarten classroom. The question is not should academic content be taught, but ***how*** that content is taught. The National Association for the Education of Young Children (NAEYC) has guidelines for Developmentally Appropriate Practice (DAP).[34] They say that young children learn best through a variety of instructional designs including large and small group instruction and play. Unfortunately, direct teacher instruction has increased greatly over the past few years. While this design can be used in small doses, over-reliance on large group instruction is an artifact of No Child Left Behind and Common Core standards and is not the best way for young children to learn.

Some children will enter kindergarten reading, some will be on the cusp of reading, and some will still be learning their letters. All will benefit from play, but all will also benefit from large group instruction such as a morning meetings to discuss the work of the day and to reinforce developing literacy and numeracy skills, and small group instruction that can target their particular skills. Children who come to kindergarten reading should be able to continue their growth as readers, and children who are just beginning to learn letters and hear sounds should receive instruction that helps them acquire these literacy abilities.

However, we must be careful to make sure that the academic focus of kindergarten does not crowd out the traditional role of kindergarten in developing children socially and emotionally. According to the NAEYC, teachers believe social and emotional learning is more important in the early years than academic learning.[35]

The new Common Core standards, which are aimed at "college and career readiness", are mute on social and emotional development, except to recognize that the standards do not address these important aspects of learning. It is interesting that much research has shown that graduating from college is more dependent on a student's social and emotional skills than academic skills.

If social and emotional learning, taught through play and targeted instruction, is crowded out of kindergarten by the Common Core standards, the nation will achieve a pyrrhic victory indeed. We neglect social and emotional learning in schools at our children's peril and at the risk of their "college readiness."

What makes a kindergarten ready for your child? Here is a checklist of some of the things to look for.

- Are classes no larger than 22 children?
- Is the teacher certified in elementary or early childhood education?
- Is play at the center of learning? Do children have the opportunity to role play in designated areas for block play, dramatic play, and playing house and office?
- Are children engaged in talk with each other and the teacher? Is there is a hum of conversation in the room?
- Does instruction take place in large and small groups and

individually?

- Do children receive instruction at their own level in reading and math?
- Do children "write" daily according to their own abilities?
- Are children read aloud to everyday?
- Do children have the opportunity to read self-selected material daily?
- Do children explore math concepts through manipulative activities like blocks and tiles?
- Is student progress assessed through teacher observation of strengths and needs, and not through paper and pencil tests?
- Do children receive explicit instruction in working cooperatively, sharing, and taking turns?
- Do children have the opportunity to express their feelings and listen to others' feelings daily?
- Are children explicitly taught how to follow classroom routines?
- Does the teacher and does the school maintain high levels of communication with the parents and school community?
- Is homework limited to a focus on parents working with their children to reinforce literacy and math concepts for no more than 30 minutes each evening?
- Is the classroom a place where all children are welcomed for what they know and can do, and where they can develop their abilities with appropriate support over time?

What should learning look like in grades 1-5?

Just as in kindergarten, instruction in the elementary grades, 1-5 must be developmentally appropriate and designed to meet the needs of young, differently developing children. At the same time, maturing children are generally ready to take on new intellectual challenges in literacy and mathematics and a solid grounding in these subjects is the hallmark of an effective elementary learning program.

Here are the some of the components of a good elementary grades program. The list is not exhaustive, but provides a basis for determining a high quality, developmentally appropriate program.

- Are classes no larger than 25 children?
- Is the teacher certified in elementary and/or early childhood education?
- Do children spend the majority of the day with the same classmates and same teacher(s)?
- Is a significant part of the day spent in hands-on learning activities?
- Is seat work (completing worksheets) kept to a minimum?
- Does instruction happen in a variety of group settings – large group, small group, partnerships, and individual instruction?
- Do children have frequent opportunities to move around the room?
- Is the classroom neat, well-organized, and colorful with lots of helpful "anchor charts" for student reference?

- Do the children have frequent opportunities to interact with other children in pairs and small groups?
- Are the children read aloud to daily?
- Do children receive daily small group reading instruction?
- Do children have the opportunity to read books of their own choice daily?
- Is the classroom well stocked with a variety of books for children to explore?
- Do children have the opportunity to write about their reading and their own experiences daily?
- Do the children receive daily instruction in writing?
- Are writing materials readily available to children?
- Are math concepts explored and reinforced with the use of math manipulatives (blocks, tiles, interlocking cubes, Cuisenaire rods, etc.)?
- Are a variety of word games, math games and other children's games available and used by the children?
- Is homework limited to no more than 30 minutes a night for primary grades (1-3) and no more than 60 minutes a night for intermediate grades (4-5), focused on reading, writing or math reinforcement?
- Are students assessed primarily through observation rather than through paper and pencil tests focused on success or failure?
- Are a variety of cultural and racial backgrounds reflected in the classroom environment, in the classroom library and

in the classroom learning materials?

- Is there good communication between the school and the home?
- Do children have frequent instruction in science and social studies?
- Do children have regularly scheduled instruction in music, art, health and physical education?
- Do the children visit the school library frequently?
- Do children have regular times for recess and free play?
- Is technology available, in good repair and used as a tool to reinforce instruction?
- Are learning supports in literacy, math, speech, occupational therapy and English as a second language readily available?

One worry that many educators and parents have expressed to me is that the new, supposedly more rigorous, Common Core standards will force a more "academic" environment on the elementary grades. There is nothing wrong with rigor as a goal in education as long as rigor is defined as asking children to work diligently to achieve learning goals that are within their reach.

However, if rigor is defined as kids sitting at their desks, reading texts that are beyond their reach, and completing endless worksheets, then we are not improving learning, we are just making learning more difficult than it needs to be and potentially turning kids off to further learning.

What does a developmentally appropriate

middle school program look like?

Middle school children are going through more rapid development than at any other period of their lives except for when they were babies. All this physical, social and emotional change creates special opportunities and requirements for a middle school program. Here are some of the things to look for in a well-thought out program for middle schools. Many of these items can be found on the California Department of Education Website, Taking Center Stage – Act II (TCSII).[36]

- Are adults and students grouped into small learning communities with stable, close and mutually respectful relationships?

- Does every student have a mentor or adviser who stays with that child throughout middle school?

- Does the school provide a wide range of support services including nurses, counselors and resource teachers to help students and families?

- Does the school learning program provide multiple opportunities for students to explore a variety of interests? This is often accomplished through mini-courses, i.e. short courses on a variety of topics.

- Is learning often inter-disciplinary? That is, students may read a piece of historical fiction in language arts that relates to the period under study in social studies and also study music of the period in a music class.

- Is homework limited to no more than 90 minutes a night?

- Does the student have the choice of a wide variety of after school activities including intra-mural and inter-mural sports?

- Is the school learning program both socially significant (deals with important issues) and personally relevant (student opinions sought and valued) to students?
- Do teachers foster creativity, curiosity and the development of social skills in a structured and supportive environment?
- Does the school deal proactively with issues of bullying and interpersonal relationships in school and in life?
- Does the school and do the teachers maintain good communication with parents?

Students in middle-school are generally ready for an environment where they change classes and where teachers are content experts in their field, but maintaining a small learning community provides a safety net for rapidly developing young minds and bodies.

What does a developmentally appropriate high school program look like?

High school students are looking for their place in society and how to proceed with their futures. They are both ready to take more responsibility for their choices and prone to risky behavior. A good high school program provides students with considerable choice in their academic program, but continues to provide guidance in making good choices. Among the choices students should have is the choice to take more academically challenging courses. Good schools provide all students the opportunity to take these courses and the support they need to be successful.

Here are some questions to ask of a high school program.

- Does the high school provide a wide range of courses in a variety of subjects, including specialized courses in science, mathematics, social studies and language arts?
- Are high level courses such as Advanced Placement and International Baccalaureate available to and promoted for ***all*** students?
- Do students have significant choices in their program of study?
- Does the school offer a rich and varied program in the performing and visual arts including theater, music, dance, film, art and photography?
- Does the school offer extensive counseling services for students including social and emotional counseling as well as college and career counseling?
- Does the school offer service learning opportunities such as internships in local hospitals, social service agencies, non-profit organizations and businesses?
- Does the school offer a rich and varied program of extra-curricular activities including clubs and athletics?
- Is homework limited to no more than 2 hours a night?
- Do the teachers communicate effectively with their students?
- Does the school and do the teachers maintain good communication with parents?

It is the local community's responsibility to provide public schools that provide these opportunities for all children. Whether a school is in a wealthy suburb, a poor rural area or a struggling urban environment, all children deserve the kinds of learning environments described here. It is the responsibility of all adults, parents, community members, policy makers and educators, to make this happen. A developmentally appropriate education is a right every child should and must enjoy.

What resources will help me learn more about developmentally appropriate practice?

For a highly informative book on the development of young children aimed at educators, but accessible for all try this:

Bodrova, E. & Leong, D. J. (2006). *Tools of the Mind*. Upper Saddle River, NJ: Prentice Hall.

For a book aimed at parents that has become a classic in the field of developmentally appropriate child rearing try this book:

Elkind, D. (2006). *The Hurried Child – 25th Anniversary Edition.* NY: De Capo Press.

For a practical, warm and witty book on child development and the benchmarks to be aware of aimed at teachers and parents try this:

Wood, C. (2007). *Yardsticks: Children in the Classroom Ages 4-14.* Turner Falls, MA: Center for Responsive Schools.

For a website devoted to the developmentally appropriate education of young children try this:

The National Association for the Education of Young Children. http://www.naeyc.org/

4

Meeting Your Child's Learning Needs in Literacy and Mathematics

How can I support my child's learning to read and write at home?

My youngest daughter, Megan, is now a wife, mother and outstanding (in her father's humble opinion) special education teacher. When she was about 5 years old, she fell in love with a wonderful picture book that I had brought home, *Tell Me a Mitzi*, by Lore Segal, with pictures by Harriet Pincus. Each night for months I would ask Megan what book she would like to read for bedtime, and each night for months her answer would be "Mitzi." Mitzi had a little brother named Jacob and for some reason Megan was fascinated by that name, which she would delightedly pronounce as if it rhymed with "hiccup" and then laugh hysterically at some joke only she understood.

Not long after this experience, Megan started school and

thankfully her literacy education proceeded smoothly. When her teacher asked her to bring in her favorite book for show and tell, she of course took in "Mitzi." As a practicing reading specialist at the time, I knew the power of story and the power of home story time on children's emerging literacy, but as a father it was fascinating to watch as Megan invited herself into the world of books through *Tell Me a Mitzi* and how a read aloud begat a love of books and how a love of books begat a life-long reader.

Years and years of research make it clear that the literacy environment in the home has a profound impact on children's literacy development once they enter school. Here are just a few of the things we know about the home/literacy connection:

- Parental involvement with reading activities at home has significant positive influence on reading achievement, language comprehension, and expressive language skills.[37]
- Parental involvement has a significant positive impact on children's interest in reading, attitudes towards reading, and attentiveness in the classroom.[38]
- Parents who promote the view that reading is a valuable and worthwhile activity have children who are motivated to read for pleasure.[39]
- The earlier parents become involved in their children's literacy practices, the more profound the results and the longer-lasting the effects.[40]

In 1983, researcher Denny Taylor coined the term "family literacy" to describe the ways in which reading and writing were embedded in the daily lives of the families she worked with. Taylor found that parents did not set out to teach literacy skills to their children, but rather encouraged their children to participate in a variety of rich and varied literacy activities.[41] Taylor's insights allow us to broaden our understanding of what a literate home environment is and to identify activities that we can do at home to invite children into the literacy club.

Below I list some of the attributes of a literate home environment. This list comes with a caution, however. Not all of these literacy practices fit seamlessly into all families and all cultures. For example, researcher Shirley Brice Heath found that the white middle-class family interactions with their children around literacy differed greatly from African American family interactions. Because the white middle-class family interactions aligned more closely to instruction that took place in school, white middle-class students tended to do better in school.[42] This observation does not mean that African American literacy practices are inferior; it means that school instructional practice needs to be more inclusive and more able to build on the literacy strengths that children of all different backgrounds bring to school. The list below, then, is suggestive and not definitive, and if some of these are absent in some home environments it does not mean that a rich literacy environment does not exist.

- **Reading is practiced by the adults in the home** – When children see that the adults closest to them read, they learn that reading is an important human activity worthy of emulation. It makes little difference what the reading material is, books, magazines, newspapers, in print or digital, as long as children see those around them reading. Adults can drive home the value of the activity by stopping to read something aloud that they found interesting or remarkable, or to share some information they learned from reading.

- **Writing is practiced by the adults in the home** – A literate household uses writing in a variety of ways. The important thing that children learn in a household where people write is that writing is a means of communication that can inform, persuade or simply serve as a memory aid. So whether it is letters, emails, grocery lists or post-it note reminders placed on the bedroom door or refrigerator, children should see writing being used to communicate and they should have writing materials readily available for their own writing attempts.

- **Literacy materials are available in the home** – When you walk into a Barnes & Noble at the mall you can barely get in the door without tripping over a display of the newest bestsellers. The home should be the same way. Literacy materials should be found throughout the home. Books on shelves and end tables, magazines on the coffee table and newspapers on the kitchen table. For children to grow as literate humans, the "stuff" of literacy must surround them.

- **Children are included and encouraged to participate in family conversations** – The greatest ally young students have in learning to read and write in school is the oral language they bring with them from home. Oral language is developed when children are seen and heard. Conversations conducted with children rather than commands directed at children help children develop the oral language they need to underpin their emerging literacy skills in school.

- **Children are read to regularly** – Reading aloud is important. Children who are read to from an early age show a greater interest in reading at later ages, have superior reading comprehension skills and have more expressive language abilities. But just as important is the talk that surrounds the read aloud. A read aloud should include frequent opportunities to talk with children about what has been read, to ask and answer questions and to talk about what a story made the child feel and/or think about.

- **Family stories** – All families have stories, such as the story of my daughter Megan and *Tell Me a Mitzi* above. Family stories are an important way for children to develop their oral language and their understanding of the narrative structure of stories. Family stories are also a good way to pass down an oral history of the family; an oral history that gives children a firm understanding of who they are and where they come from.

- **Family library trips** – Regular whole family trips to the library reinforce the importance of literacy and provide children with a wide array of literacy materials on a wide variety of topics to explore. Many public libraries also have a story time for young children. All members of the family should have a library card and should use it regularly.

- **Family trips to museums, cultural events and historical landmarks** – Reading comprehension is built on broad knowledge of multiple topics. Regular family visits to art, history and science museums, and zoos help build knowledge that can be applied to reading and learning in the classroom. For younger children, museums that offer "hands-on" activities offer the best learning opportunities. Many museums offer special programs for children of varying age groups.

- **Sharing a fascination with words** – All of the activities described above will help children develop a rich vocabulary, but parents can also help with vocabulary development by being on the lookout for interesting, exciting, curious words that pop-up in reading or in conversation, and by simply talking about words used by characters on TV or written on billboards or restaurant menus. We want to develop a "word consciousness" in children – a fascination with words and their many and varied uses. When parents see interesting words, they should talk about them with their children.

- **Combine TV watching with talk** – Television is not the enemy of literacy learning. Television viewing can be educational, whether kids are watching something that is informative or merely watching an entertaining cartoon or sitcom. The key to making TV watching a literate experience is talk. During commercials the TV can be muted and parents and children can talk about what they have seen and predict what they will happen next. At the end of the program, the TV can be turned off and the family can discuss what they have seen, summarize the big ideas and family members can share what stood out for them in the show.

- **Turn the television captions on** – All TVs are now required to have caption capability. Originally developed to help the hearing impaired enjoy television, it has since been discovered that captions help students develop important literacy skills. As Cynthia Mershon notes in an article for the *Russ on Reading* blog:

  > *Research…reveals that when students read the words on the television screen and hear them spoken by the people in the television program or movie and see the pictures or images on the television screen that tell them what those words mean, their reading comprehension, vocabulary, fluency, and general engagement with reading increases and develops at a higher rate than those students not watching captioned television. In particular, learning disabled and ESL students exhibit dramatic improvement in*

language skills when captioned television is a regular part of their reading program.[43]

- **Continue all of these practices after children begin school** – Once children begin school and begin to formally learn to read and write, good home literacy practices, including read aloud, should continue in the home. Continued emphasis on literacy in the home supports the work of the classroom teacher and the continuing learning efforts of your child.

What kinds of reading and writing instruction should I see in the classroom?

The teaching of literacy has been the topic of much debate over the years. The "reading wars" as they have been called, are essentially an argument over whether a heavy emphasis on decoding (breaking down words into their component sounds) or an emphasis on meaning (comprehending what is read) is the one true path to literacy success. In the end this is a false debate because both are necessary for creating life-long readers and literacy development is much more complex than these two feuding camps would suggest.

It is interesting that no matter what reading program is used, most children learn to read pretty well. There are exceptions, of course, and many children do have difficulty in learning to read. Some children will need special interventions to help them on the way to literacy, but for most the instructional program does not make much difference, at least as far as reading proficiency is concerned.

What does make a difference is an emphasis on not just developing the skill of the reader, but also attending to the will of the reader. If children learn how to read, yet find no joy in reading and therefore do not choose to read, then the skill is of little consequence. As Mark Twain once said, "The person who can read and does not has no advantage over the person who cannot read." Thoughtful teachers attend to both the **skill** and the **will** of the developing reader.

What parents should be looking for and what schools and teachers should be offering is a balanced approach to literacy. A balanced approach offers children the decoding instruction they need within the structure of real reading situations. Decoding is important, but it is best learned as a contributing factor to the real purpose of reading, which is to get meaning. There can be no reading comprehension without decoding, yet decoding is assisted greatly by the reader's search to make sense of the reading material. Skillful teachers offer students the decoding instruction they need based on their performance in real reading situations, and guide the students in developing problem solving strategies that help them use all the sources of information available to them to read and understand a text.

So what does this look like in the classroom? In reading instruction the following should be happening in all elementary classrooms:

- Children are read aloud to daily.
- Children receive direct instruction in some reading strategy/skill daily.
- Children have the time to practice their reading skills in a book of their own choosing daily.
- Children do word work activities daily
- Children have regular opportunities (3-5 times a week) to read in small groups under the guidance of the teacher.

Word work includes such activities as a word wall for developing sight vocabulary, making words activities where students arrange and rearrange letters to make words of varying length, guessing the covered word where students learn to predict words and confirm their predictions as letters are uncovered, and word sorts where children sort words into different letter and spelling patterns (may, say, day) (cat, bat, rat). Word work for older children will focus on decoding multi-syllable words and vocabulary development.

A balanced approach to writing instruction takes a similar approach. Children should have the following experiences in writing in the classroom daily:

- Direct instruction in some writing skill/strategy.
- Opportunity to "tryout" the new skill/strategy.
- Opportunity to write on a self-selected topic.
- Regular opportunities to confer with other students and the teacher about writing.
- Opportunity to share writing with others and listen to each other's writing.

A balanced literacy classroom is festooned with "anchor charts" that provide reminders for children on such topics as "How to Choose a 'Just Right' Book" or "Things to Do During Reading Time" or "How to Punctuate Dialogue in a Story." Lots of books should be available in the classroom and they should be easy to find. There should be comfortable places for kids to read independently and lots of print at eye level (like the word wall) for the children to use for help when they need it.

Assessment of the children should be done, for the most part, through teacher observation and documentation. Reading and writing are skills to be developed, not content subjects where knowledge is to be learned and tested. The focus of assessment should be on what progress is being shown and what next steps are necessary. Teachers should be able to tell parents if their child is on, above or below expectations for his/her age and grade level and what the plans are for future literacy development.

What kinds of progress in literacy should I see from my child over time?

Normal progression in reading is fairly easy for a parent to track. Just as children develop teeth and learn to speak at different ages, reading development is individual and some children will read earlier than others, but just as all children eventually get teeth, so, too, do most children move in a fairly predictable pattern toward reading.

Perhaps the easiest way to tell if your child is progressing normally in reading is to look at the size of the print in the books that s/he is reading. As print gets smaller, as more words appear on a page, children are advancing in their reading. By the end of second grade most children are reading simple chapter books and by the end of fourth grade children are reading novels for young readers. Progress is generally rapid and easy to spot in the primary grades and less obvious as students move to more fluent (and silent) reading.

Here are some benchmarks in reading and writing to look for along the way:

By the end of kindergarten –

- Holds book correctly, turns pages left to right.

- Knows 15-30 sight words (words that can be read quickly and easily on sight).
- Hears sounds in words (c-a-t in cat).
- Hears rhyming words.
- Knows the alphabet.
- Begins to track words on the page with finger.
- Can identify a known word on a page.
- Can identify an unknown word on a page.
- Reads simple books with highly recognizable patterns and supportive pictures.
- Enjoys being read to and reading/pretend reading books.
- Can retell a story after listening to it.
- Writes some words correctly.
- Likes to talk out what s/he is preparing to write.
- Generally draws a picture and then includes some words in writing.
- Uses invented spelling* when writing words that are not yet known.
- Can tell the message s/he was writing, although it may not be recognizable to adults.
- Benchmark Book: Some children will be reading by the end of kindergarten, while others will not be; therefore, I do not suggest a benchmark book for kindergarten. If children are able to do the things listed above, they will be ready for reading instruction in grade 1. Programs that call

for all kindergarteners to be reading at a certain level before entering first grade are misguided.

By the end of grade 1 –

- All of the above skills for kindergarten are in place.
- Has a continually growing sight word vocabulary.
- Can break apart words with simple patterns (sit, back, start, help).
- Recognizes word families (may, say, way, day) (flight, sight, might, fright, right).
- Tracks words on the page with eyes and without finger pointing.
- Notices when s/he makes an error, and tries to fix it.
- Can retell a story with details after reading.
- Reads picture books of increasing length and complexity, with more words on the page and less support from pictures.
- Enjoys being read to.
- Reads books of his/her own choosing with increasing fluency. (Fluency is the smooth, rapid processing of print. In other words, the child reads the words so they sound like talking).
- Talks about what will be written before writing.
- Moves from drawing and writing to writing and then illustrating.
- Uses a mix of correctly spelled words and invented spelling* to write stories

- Sustains writing over several sentences.
- Benchmark Book: *Hattie and the Fox,* by Mem Fox.

By the end of grade 2 –

- All of the above skills for first grade and kindergarten.
- Has a continually growing store of sight words.
- Identifies words with irregular vowel patterns (noise, brown, weigh).
- Identifies many two and three-syllable words.
- Notices when s/he makes an error and has strategies to fix it.
- Can retell a story using narrative structure.
- Learns new information from reading informational text.
- Reads simple chapter books with little or no picture support.
- Reads aloud fluently and with expression.
- Reads silently.
- Enjoys being read to.
- Reads a variety of books of his/her own choosing including non-fiction, picture books and simple chapter books.
- Identifies certain authors as favorites.
- Writes in response to reading.
- Can do some individual planning before writing.
- Is very aware of conventions of writing like spelling, capitalization and punctuation, but uses them imperfectly.

- Writes stories with a beginning, middle, and end.
- Revises work by adding on to story.
- Spells most words in stories correctly, but continues to use invented spelling* for unknown words.
- Benchmark Book: *The Secret of the Polk Street School*, Patricia Reilly Giff.

By the end of grade 3 –

- All of the above skills for grades K-2.
- Has a continually growing store of sight words.
- Identifies words with 3, 4 and 5 syllables.
- Uses a variety of strategies to correct errors in reading.
- Reads a variety of picture and chapter books, both fiction and non-fiction, of his/her own choosing.
- Enjoys being read to.
- Identifies a growing number of authors as favorites.
- Reads increasingly challenging books with fluency and expression.
- Writes in response to reading.
- Plans writing before writing a draft.
- Spells most words correctly and tries to correct those that are not known.
- Writes longer stories with a beginning, middle, and end.
- Edits work for correctness.

- Revises stories to add information.
- Writes informational reports.
- Writes short persuasive pieces.
- Benchmark Book: *Stone Fox*, James Reynolds Gardiner.

By the end of grades 4 and 5 –

- All of the above skills for grades K-3.
- Identifies most multiple syllable words.
- Determines the meaning of new and unfamiliar words from their context, by asking someone or by looking them up.
- Builds vocabulary through reading more and more complex texts.
- Reads increasingly challenging books with fluency and expression.
- Reads a variety of fiction and non-fiction texts designed for developing readers.
- Enjoys being read to.
- Reads for pleasure and to gain new information.
- Uses information gained from reading in writing.
- Writes in response to reading.
- Plans writing before writing a draft.
- Spells most words correctly and tries to correct those that are not known.
- Attempts longer and more complex sentence structures.

- Edits work for correctness.
- Revises work for greater clarity.
- Writes longer stories with a beginning, middle and end.
- Writes informational reports and persuasive pieces
- Benchmark book grade 4: *The Whipping Boy*, Sid Fleischman.
- Benchmark book grade 5: *The Sign of the Beaver*, Elizabeth George Speare.

By the end of grades 6,7,8 –

- All of the above skills for K-5.
- Reads for pleasure and to gain information.
- Uses information gained from reading in research reports.
- Enjoys being read to.
- Reads a variety of fiction and non-fiction texts of increasing difficulty.
- Develops strategies for reading textbook information.
- Identifies particular authors as favorites.
- Uses information gained from reading in writing.
- Plans writing before writing a draft.
- Spells most words correctly and corrects those that are not known.
- Successfully uses a variety of sentence lengths and complexities.

- Revises work for greater clarity.
- Develops a clear voice in writing.
- Edits work for correctness.
- Writes in response to reading.
- Writes literary analysis, informational reports and persuasive pieces.
- Benchmark book grade 6: *A Girl Named Disaster*, Nancy Farmer.
- Benchmark book grade 7: *My Brother Sam is Dead,* James Lincoln Collier and Christopher Collier.
- Benchmark book grade 8: *The Outsiders,* S.E. Hinton.

By the end of grades 9, 10, 11, 12 –

- All of the above skills for K-8
- Reads for pleasure and to gain new information.
- Uses a variety of strategies to read and gain information from textbooks.
- Reads technical articles and other informative to research a variety of subjects.
- Uses reading as a tool for research into topics of interest.
- Enjoys being read to.
- Builds technical vocabulary through reading.
- Plans writing before writing a draft.
- Spells most words correctly and corrects those that are not

known.

- Successfully uses a variety of sentence lengths and complexities.
- Revises work for greater clarity.
- Edits work for correctness.
- Writes in response to reading.
- Writes literary analysis, informational reports and persuasive pieces.
- Uses writing as a tool to explain and clarify ideas and to persuade others.
- Benchmark book grade 9: *Of Mice and Men*, John Steinbeck
- Benchmark book grade 10: *To Kill a Mockingbird*, Harper Lee.
- Benchmark book for grade 11: *The Great Gatsby*, F. Scott Fitzgerald.
- Benchmark book for grade 12: *The Handmaid's Tale,* Margaret Atwood.

*Invented spelling – the practice of spelling unfamiliar words by making an educated guess as to the correct spelling based on the writer's existing knowledge of the sounds that letters make in a word (*bak* for back, *dinasor* for dinosaur). Invented spelling is employed in the early grades because it helps students learn to decode by listening for sounds in words and it also allows students to write with greater fluency without stopping to look up every third word they write.

What can I do if my child struggles in reading and writing?

First of all, don't panic. Many children exhibit some delays in learning to read and write. Research indicates that most children catch up by about fourth grade. If you have concerns, the best thing to do is to talk to your child's classroom teacher. First find out if the teacher shares your concern. If the teacher does not have the same concerns, ask questions to help you understand what is going on.

If the teacher does share the concern, work with the teacher on a plan for improvement. Improvement plans should be based on both the strengths and the weaknesses your child exhibits. Using your child's strengths is a good way to help him/her overcome weaknesses. Most reading difficulties fall into two categories: (1) difficulty with fluency – the smooth and accurate decoding of the words on the page; or (2) difficulty comprehending what was read.

If children understand stories that are read aloud to them, but struggle with decoding words, the strength in comprehension can be used to help them develop better fluency. Teachers will prompt students to look at words and think about what would look right, sound right and make sense. Over time most children improve in their ability to decode words. One of the best ways to improve decoding ability is by rereading familiar stories. Parents can help here by listening to their children read over again short stories and poems that they have read in school. For struggling readers it is often helpful for the parent to share the reading load, alternating pages with the child and thus lightening the load on the developing reader.

If your child generally reads with good fluency, but struggles in retelling what was read or in answering questions about what was read, the strength in decoding can be used to develop better comprehension. As children read aloud to the teacher, the teacher will stop the reader and ask for a quick retelling. Stopping along the way will communicate to the reader that s/he must think about what is going on in the story as s/he reads. Some students also need to learn to "read the punctuation." That is, slow down for periods, commas and other marks that help the reader understand what is happening.

Parents can help with comprehension difficulties by reading together with their child and stopping at various points to talk about what is going on, and sharing their own understandings. Reading comprehension is a thinking activity. All thinking activities can help students with reading comprehension. So, besides reading and talking about books, watching a TV show together and then turning off the TV and discussing what happened can help children develop their reading comprehension.

Most children who struggle with reading also struggle with writing, and some children who are progressing well in reading still struggle in writing. If you are concerned about your child's writing progress, you should again bring these concerns up with the teacher, find out what s/he has observed, and develop a plan of action. The best way to help your child in writing is by being a good audience for the writing. If the child has something to write at home, it is a good idea with younger children to talk with them about what they will write before the writing takes place, and then leave the child alone to write. Sometimes a child may be concerned about the spelling of some words, so a parent can help by writing down these "tricky" words for before the child writes. For other children it may be helpful to jot down the ideas as they are shared, providing the child with an outline to use for writing.

When the child has finished, ask that the writing be read aloud to you. By listening to your child read the writing, you will focus on the message and the quality of what is being said rather than on the spelling and punctuation. Provide your child with feedback on the message that is being communicated before commenting on the mechanics of how it was written.

After focusing on the content of the message, sit down with your child to see what has been written and assist with spelling and punctuation. Most of the time it is more helpful to tell your child how to spell the word. A dictionary is a very clunky tool as an aid in spelling, so use it sparingly and help your child to look up a word rather than abandoning him/her to look it up on his/her own.

Of course, for some children more help is needed. If your child does not seem to be making adequate progress despite the good efforts of the teacher and you at home, other steps need to be taken. A process like Response to Intervention (RTI), described in detail in Chapter 2, should be in place to make sure your child is getting the support required. Sometimes a school will recommend a "basic skills support program", where your child will receive extra literacy instruction, either in the regular classroom with a specially trained teacher or in a small group outside of the regular classroom. Children who exhibit ongoing difficulties in reading and writing may be provided with a special education teacher, again either in or out of the regular classroom, to provide intensive instruction in areas of need.

As the parent, you should be well informed about any of these steps and should have input into any instructional program designed for your child. No one program designed for students with difficulties in literacy learning has been demonstrated to work for all children. The most important factor is the teacher working with your child and the support you provide at home. Any special support program needs to be regularly reviewed to ensure that progress is being made and that it is meeting your child's needs.

When your child struggles in literacy learning, one option that your school may offer and that you may wish to explore is one-to-one tutoring. Tutoring can be effective is some cases. In my experience the most effective tutoring must be regular, more than once a week and delivered by a certified teacher. One good option is summer tutoring. Children who struggle in literacy often suffer from "summer loss." That is, they lose some of the gains they made during the school year because they are not receiving instruction in the summer. A good summer literacy tutoring program can be very helpful in combatting summer loss.

What should I do if my kid can't spell?

Of all the topics of concern I have been asked about by parents over my years as a literacy specialist, spelling is number one by far. I suppose this is because spelling errors are so visible and easy to spot. Reading errors are harder to see because they mostly happen in the reader's mind, but spelling errors are out there for all to see.

In order to reduce spelling anxiety, I think there are a few facts about spelling that all parents need to know:

1. Spelling is not related to intelligence. Many very smart people don't spell well. Albert Einstein was a rotten speller.

2. Spelling proceeds through regular developmental stages beginning with regularly spelled single syllable words (cat, bit), moving to irregularly spelled single syllable words (noise, weigh), proceeding to multi-syllable words (battle, motel) and finally to low frequency words, often derived from Greek or Latin (pneumonia, misogyny).

3. Early readers and writers benefit from approximating the

spelling of words in their writing (invented spelling). All writers, even adults, approximate spellings of unfamiliar words.

4. Good spelling is primarily a function of good visual memory. Good spellers create a mental picture of a word through their reading and replicate that when they write. That is why when asked to spell a word, we often write it down to see if it looks right.

5. Some children and adults do not have a strong visual memory and are, therefore, not strong spellers.

6. Most good spellers are also good readers, but not all good readers are good spellers.

7. Studying ten random words for a spelling test at the end of the week does not improve spelling in real world situations.

8. Poor spellers need to develop strategies to overcome this problem, These strategies include writing drafts of communication and then checking the spelling and using spelling aids such as the dictionary and computer spell checking.

When working with your own children, it is a good idea to lower the spelling anxiety and provide understanding and support. Remember that using approximate or invented spellings is a normal part of the writing process. But we also want kids to develop a spelling conscience – an awareness that spelling matters. Children should be held accountable to spell correctly words that they already know how to spell and words that they can easily find in the classroom. By grade three children should be held responsible to correct their spelling on written work that is to be turned in.

What is dyslexia? How do I know if my child has this learning disability?

Dyslexia is a learning difficulty that mainly affects the way people read and spell words. Dyslexia may be mild, moderate or severe. It is a neurological disorder impacting a person's ability to discriminate sounds in words, remember a sequence of verbal information, and process verbal information rapidly. Dyslexia is not tied to a person's general level of intelligence, although it may make learning new information through reading a challenge.

Dyslexia is a term that is surrounded by much misinformation and mythology. Some parents and even some educators have taken to using the word as a catchall for any reading disability. It is important to remember that while most children who are dyslexic have some difficulties learning to read, not all children who have reading difficulties are dyslexic.

There are many factors that may impact a child's normal reading development that are not neurological in nature, including of course, socio-economic status, literacy experiences in the home, and the quality of instruction in school.

Dyslexia is not a disease and it cannot be cured. While many theories exist about the cause of dyslexia, most scientists now generally agree that dyslexia is genetic, passed down in families. Putting a definitive number on the prevalence of dyslexia is difficult because so often dyslexia goes undiagnosed or misdiagnosed, but again experts estimate about 4% to 8% of the population are afflicted. And while dyslexia may cause many problems in learning to read and write, most dyslexics are capable of becoming very competent readers and writers.

Many of the signs of dyslexia are also displayed by normally developing children, so it is best to be cautious when looking for these signs in your own children. Pre-school children may exhibit language delays, jumble up words or phrases in their speech or have problems expressing their ideas orally.

Once in school children may have difficulty learning the letters of the alphabet, hearing rhymes in words, matching the sounds of words to letter symbols (phonics), answering questions well orally and learning sequences. The classic "symptom" for dyslexia, the reversal of letters and numbers, is actually a quite normal part of development for children up to age nine or so.

Dyslexia can be diagnosed early on and while it cannot be cured, systematic instruction and accommodations can minimize the negative effects. Interestingly, while difficulty learning phonics is a sign of possible dyslexia, according to researchers at the University of Michigan increased phonics instruction will not help dyslexics because their difficulty lies in discerning the underlying sounds of language (phonemic awareness).[44]

Because dyslexia appears to many to be a letter-sound processing problem, many commercial programs designed to treat dyslexia focus on a rigid phonics focused instructional model. This model ignores what we know about the ways that children construct meaning as they read, and ultimately may make it harder for the struggling reader to read and understand.

Treatment of dyslexia should not be based on some "one size fits all" program. Treatment should be individualized and based on your child's needs and interests. The instructor should work with you and your child to set achievement goals, with regular reporting dates for assessing progress toward the goals.[45] Most importantly, the construction of meaning (the real reason we all read) should remain central to the instructional design for the dyslexic reader.[46]

How can I support my child's mathematical understanding at home?

Just as parents can have a great influence on their children's growing understanding of how language works, parents can help their children develop underlying mathematical concepts that will help them in school. The key is to talk about the math around you to help children build awareness, and to ask questions as a springboard to discussion and investigation. Math explorations should be fun, taking on the characteristics of play and problem solving.

With very young children, make sure that they have lots of small objects (nothing they can put in their mouths!), like blocks and pop-it beads to play with. These items help children develop spatial sense, number sense, and counting skills.

Children also need to learn one-to-one correspondence. That is, the understanding that the number 1 stands for one object. Children demonstrate one-to-one correspondence when they can point to individual items when counting, 1..2..3.. and so forth. Parents can also aid their younger children by helping them notice numbers in the environment – on the front door, on the clock, on the telephone, in the grocery store and by talking about why those numbers are there.

As children get a bit older and begin their schooling, parents can help them to develop a sense of the real life applications of math. Questions about money, distance, length, weight and time can be particularly helpful. It is also important to help children develop the ability to estimate an approximate answer. Math specialist and former elementary school teacher Bob Krech suggests these questions: [47]

Money –

- How many ways can you think of to make change for a dollar?
- If something costs $1.57 and I have only one dollar bills, what should I give the cashier? How much will I get back in change?
- How much do you think it will cost to eat at McDonald's? How about at Ruby Tuesday's?
- If a pound of grapes costs $4.00, what will two pounds cost?

Distance/Length –

- How long do you think the dashboard of the car is? How about the whole car?
- How far away is the couch from the TV?
- What would be about a mile from our house?
- How far do you think it is around your head? How could you find out for sure?
- I want to measure the length of my tooth. What unit of measurement would be best to use: Feet? Inches? Centimeters? Millimeters?

Weight –

- How much do you think this box of cereal weighs?
- Do you weigh more than our dog? How much more?
- What do you think five baseballs/eggs/shoes would weigh?
- How would you weigh a cotton ball?

Time –

- If you started walking and you walked for five minutes, how far do you think you would get?
- Can you hop on one foot for a minute? Can you stand on one foot for a minute?
- What time do you need to get up to be ready for school? When do you leave for school? How long does it take us to get ready for school?
- How many minutes/hours a week do you think we spend eating? Sleeping? Watching TV? How could you find out for sure?

Operations and Number Sense –

- How many do you think 7 groups of 26 might be?
- Would 29 plus 47 be more than 100?
- Can you spot five numbers on the way to school? What are they?
- What is the highest number you can find written in our house? The lowest?
- Why is the radio station called 98.3?

Estimation –

- How many blueberries are in this package?
- How long will it take us to drive to your school?
- What would you guess is the length and width of your room?
- How much water did you use to take your bath?

What kinds of mathematics instruction should I see in the classroom?

Every day in every classroom children should be solving problems. These could be word problems or project type problems (what is the square footage in our classroom?), but they all should involve applying math skills and using them. Children should also have an opportunity to discuss different ways to solve problems and be invited to explain their thinking both verbally and in writing. Students should have the opportunity to work both on their own and in small groups.

Just as a balanced approach to literacy is the wisest course, so too in math. Mastery of facts (addition, subtraction, multiplication) is important, but children still need to be thinking through math problems even before they have mastered all the facts. Underlying understanding of math concepts helps in the mastery of facts, just as the mastery of facts aids in the efficient solving of problems. In other words, memorizing 7 times 7 equals 49 is useful, but such memorization is aided by the underlying understanding and ability to visualize that 7 times 7 means 7 groups of 7 objects. And the practical application of multiplication, in this example perhaps quickly determining the number of seats in a room, makes the utility of mastering the facts clear.

In the classroom students should constantly be encouraged to explain why something works the way it does in mathematics. For example, when we multiply ½ by 4, why is it that we get an answer (2) that is smaller than 4, even though we are multiplying? Teachers who encourage this type of thinking as a central part of their math instruction are helping children master facts through a deeper understanding of how math works.[48]

What kind of progress in mathematics should I see from my child over time?

Children should develop a variety of strategies for solving problems and doing mathematical operations. Over time, they should develop perseverance in solving problems. In order for this to happen, parents (and teachers) need to step back and let kids struggle with challenging work. There is more than one way to add (87 + 53). As children progress in ability, we should see them developing a repertoire of strategies for solving problems.

Children should also develop core math knowledge such as knowing addition facts automatically, the multiplication tables, and that there are 12 inches in a foot, 3 feet in a yard, etc. Children should be continually expanding their ability to read, write, understand, and manipulate larger numbers as they move forward.[49]

What can I do if my child struggles in mathematics?

If you sense your child is struggling in math, or if your child voices a concern, the first step is to contact the teacher for a face to face conference. The teacher can help you understand what the expectations of the class are and clarify any difficulties the child might be having. Some children need more time and more repetition to master math concepts. Working with the teacher, you might develop a plan where you can preview new material at home, giving your child a "leg up" on the upcoming instruction, and/or the teacher may suggest practice activities you can do at home to reinforce classroom instruction.

Math expert and parent Bob Krech says,

> *Do not fall into the trap of having [children] drill and drill and memorize procedures. This will only help in the short term. When [children] then have to think and apply these concepts, [rote learning] will all fall apart. Usually, more time on task is the best remedy.*[50]

What should I do if I feel my child is not being appropriately challenged in school?

Of all the parent concerns I fielded during my time as a school district administrator the most frequent was, "My child is not being challenged." In order to learn and acquire new skills in school, children must be challenged to go beyond what they already know and are able to do. The key for the teacher is finding the appropriate level of challenge, because just as some challenge is necessary, too much challenge can shut down learning as well. What is that "just right" level? The answer, of course, is that it is different for every child, and thus finding the right level of challenge for each child is a major challenge for the teacher.

It is interesting that the symptoms of too little challenge are very similar to the symptoms of too much challenge: complaints of being bored, inattention, daydreaming and distractibility.[51] So it is important to pay close attention to what your child is saying about school and to what the teacher is reporting to you about your child's learning and behavior. If homework turns into a battle of wills at home and your child gets easily frustrated or says s/he doesn't understand, your child may be feeling over-challenged. If your child reports during homework time that the work is really easy and therefore boring, you might want to check into the level of challenge. Homework should be fairly easy because it is meant to be completed without the aid of the teacher, and should provide reinforcement of concepts already taught. Still, if your child is complaining work is too easy, you should listen and investigate.

Sometimes kids may complain of being bored or of the work being too easy because they don't understand what a teacher is aiming for in the instruction, which may be more complex than the child realizes. For example, children may feel that items on a spelling test are too easy or words they already know, but the teacher may be shooting for students to develop knowledge about the way words work that they can apply more universally. For example the teacher might ask students to spell a list of words like *sign, signal, assignment, signature, significant, assignation, signatory, signet.* A good speller might think many of these words are "easy", but the teacher might be helping children to see that all the words are related based on the root word "sign" and even when the "g" is silent it stays in the spelling of the word to help readers understand the meaning.

Likewise in math, students may feel they already know how to solve problems the teacher assigns. But the teacher may be working to get to the underlying principles that allow math problems to be solved in certain ways. So while a student may be able to quickly and easily demonstrate how to multiply two numbers, the teacher is looking for an understanding that multiplication is not just a shortcut, but a set of numerical relationships that forms the basis for understanding many algebraic equations. For example, children may say, "I already know that 7 times 6 equals 42", but a teacher may be looking for deeper understanding and application of this knowledge by asking questions like, "What makes you think that is true? Can you show me proof that it is true using a picture or diagram or related number fact? Can you show me another way to do this? When might you use this fact? Can you write a word problem where the reader would have to use this fact to solve it?"

While teachers should be making underlying understandings clear to children, sometimes what appears to be easy for some kids is really just a reinforcement that is directed at deeper understanding.

What resources will help me learn more about my child's learning needs?

For books on developing language and literacy in young children, try these:

Bialostok, S. (1992). *Raising Readers: Helping Your Child to Literacy.* Manitoba, Canada: Peguis Publishers.

Duke, N. and Bennett-Armistead, V. S. (2014). *Beyond Bedtime Stories, 2nd. Edition: A Parent's Guide to Promoting Reading Writing, and Other Literacy Skills from Birth to 5.* NYC: Scholastic.

Lathey, N. and Blake, T. (2014). *Small Talk: How to Develop Your Child's Language Skills from Birth to Age Four.* NYC: The Experiment.

For books on the power of reading aloud with suggestions on how to conduct read aloud at home see:

Allyn, P. (2009). *What to Read When: The Books and Stories to Read with Your Child--and All the Best Times to Read Them.* Garden City, NY: Avery.

Trelease, J. (2013). *The Read Aloud Handbook, Seventh Edition.* NYC: Penguin Books.

For a book on reading and writing development for adolescents, try this:

Fleischer, C. (2010). *Reading and Writing and Teens: A Parent's Guide to Adolescent Literacy.* NYC: NCTE.

For a series of books that can help you help your child with math learning and math homework try this series from Great Source Publishing:

Math to Learn (K-2)
Math to Know (2-5)
Math at Hand (5-6)
Math on Call (6-8)
Algebra to Go (7-12)
Geometry to Go (7-12)

Another great series to help with addition, subtraction, multiplying and dividing is:

Leutzinger, L. (2002). *Facts that Last.* Columbus, OH: McGraw-Hill.

For a website to help you answer many math questions, which includes an "Ask Dr. Math" feature go here:

Math Forum. http://mathforum.org.

You can read more about dyslexia, myths, reality and treatment here:

NHS Choices. (n.d.). *Dyslexia Symptoms.* http://www.nhs.uk/Conditions/Dyslexia/Pages/Symptoms.aspx

Dyslexia Help. (2015). *Principles of Effective Dyslexia Intervention.* University of Michigan. http://dyslexiahelp.umich.edu/parents/learn-about-dyslexia/dyslexia-treatment/principles-effective-dyslexia-treatment

Dyslexia Help. (2015). *Debunking Common Myths about Dyslexia.* University of Michigan. http://dyslexiahelp.umich.edu/dyslexics/learn-about-dyslexia/what-is-dyslexia/debunking-common-myths-about-dyslexia

5

Meeting Your Child's Social and Emotional Needs

Today's educators have a renewed perspective on what common sense always suggested: when schools attend systematically to students' social and emotional skills, the academic achievement of children increases, the incidence of problem behaviors decreases, and the quality of the relationships surrounding each child improves.[52]

What is social and emotional education and why does it matter?

In his 1996 book, *Emotional Intelligence*, Daniel Goleman says that social and emotional intelligence is a "different way of being smart."[53] Social and emotional education aims at helping kids be smart in self-management, in problem solving and decision making, in understanding themselves, in relationships with others, and in their work and play. Social and emotional education is not so much a separate curriculum, although it is addressed that way in many schools, but a way of teaching and guiding student development that is embedded in all school activities. Social and emotional learning (SEL) may be addressed through classroom instruction, through extra-curricular activities, through a supportive school climate and through community service projects.

Research indicates that an explicit and deliberate approach to social and emotional learning is directly related to student academic achievement. The Carnegie Council on Adolescent Development found that the common denominator in effective middle schools was a well-designed program for social and emotional learning. Programs included such things as mentoring programs, group guidance and counseling sessions, creative approaches to discipline issues, and classroom time dedicated to social and emotional skill building.[54] Other research has demonstrated that social and emotional factors are more important to a successful high school to college transition and graduation from college than are scores on standardized tests.[55]

What are the school's and the teacher's responsibilities in meeting my child's social and emotional needs?

Schools may address SEL directly by providing a variety of instructional programs aimed at character education, promoting good health habits, and by sponsoring substance abuse prevention and anti-bullying campaigns. While programs like these are important, more important is the indirect social learning that occurs in a school through the healthy climate that is promoted in the classrooms, hallways, bathrooms, cafeteria and buses. Schools with a healthy climate work actively to make sure that all adults who interact with children, professional and para-professional (like cafeteria aides and bus drivers), are trained to assist students and respond to their needs in supportive, empathetic ways.

Schools that support students' social and emotional learning are staffed to meet student needs. Adequate supervision is provided for students in hallways, playgrounds, cafeterias and buses. Guidance counselors are available to work with students individually and in small groups on the many and varied needs children might have. Many schools have guidance counselor led groups for children dealing with anger issues, shyness, misbehavior and divorce. Middle and high schools often have a Substance Abuse Counselor (SAC) on staff; a person who is specially trained to work with students who may be struggling with drug and alcohol issues.

Teachers promote the social and emotional health of the students in their classrooms by building positive relationships with children as individuals, by providing an outlet for students to share their feelings, concerns and opinions, and by structuring the learning environment so that all children can feel safe, secure and successful. Social and emotional learning in the classroom should be both deliberate and a by-product of the instructional environment.

Teachers know that knowledge of their students as human beings as well as learners aids in developing lessons that meet student needs. The process is deliberate, but often fully integrated into the class work. Teachers get to know their students through surveys, formal and informal discussions, learning conferences, and through their written work.

One highly respected and research based approach to social and emotional learning is called *Responsive Classroom.* Responsive Classroom is an approach to teaching and learning that helps teachers learn to create a positive learning community, an effective management system, engaging lessons, and developmentally appropriate classroom practices. A centerpiece of the Responsive

Classroom approach is the Morning Meeting. In a Morning Meeting students learn the etiquette of greeting each other by name to start a new day, share information, participate in a brief group activity, and write a short message interactively with the teacher to identify the focus for the day.[56]

As an administrator, teacher and parent, I have been very impressed with the training and implementation of the Responsive Classroom, but whether it is a formal program or practices integrated into the instructional day, it is a teacher's responsibility to meet students' social and emotional needs as well as their intellectual needs.

What does effective school discipline look like in a school?

School discipline policies are best seen as a part of the school's social and emotional learning curriculum. Orderly classrooms, hallways and meeting areas are necessary for a positive learning environment. Therefore, schools need to develop discipline policies that promote good order. The best discipline policies reflect the input of parents, students, teachers and staff. School discipline policies should be clear, developmentally appropriate, equitable and fair, with consistent expectations and consequences. Discipline approaches should be pro-active, seeking to provide a positive learning environment that keeps the need for discipline to a minimum.

Discipline policies that rely on shaming students in front of their peers must be avoided. These policies work directly against developing the kind of inclusive and productive learning environment that schools try to create. Charter schools have popularized the notion of a "no excuses" discipline policy that often manifests itself in shaming practices, such as having students wear clothing that indicates they have broken a rule, or by separating students from their peers in the classroom and cafeteria. These measures are often enforced for minor offenses like failure to attend to the teacher in class, or speaking while in line in the hallway. These policies, often applied to poor, minority students in inner city schools, are an inappropriate use of discipline in order to coerce compliance. They are also ultimately self-defeating, creating resentful or grudgingly compliant students rather than independent thinkers.

Likewise, "zero tolerance" policies, intended for cases where students bring weapons or drugs to school, have often been applied to lesser offenses like bullying or swearing, where they fail because they preclude the use of human judgement in the discipline policy. Like all school activities, discipline requires that human beings, in this case trained teachers and administrators, be allowed to use their best judgment in applying appropriate discipline.[57]

Finally, discipline that removes the child from the learning environment, such as in-school or out-of-school suspension, should be a measure of last resort. Removing a child from school cuts that child off from the mission of the school, and is an indication of institutional failure. It also contributes significantly to the likelihood that the child will have continued discipline issues and will drop out of school. Dropping out of school triples the likelihood that a student will eventually end up in prison.[58]

What should I do if I have concerns about whether my child's social and emotional needs are not being met?

Children, of course, differ in their levels of interest and engagement in school, but all children should feel safe and secure in school and view school as a generally positive experience. If your child is consistently reluctant to go to school, doesn't like to talk about what is going on at school, or is unusually quiet or withdrawn when returning home from school, you should investigate. The first person to contact in these cases is the teacher. What is the classroom teacher seeing? Is your child participating in class, attending to instruction and apparently happy to be there? If not, what has the teacher seen that may be causing the child to be disengaged?

If the teacher is not seeing the same concerns, ask that the teacher watch for signs of your concerns and report back to you after a week or two about how things are going. If you and the teacher agree that some behaviors are of concern, work together to create a plan to improve your child's feelings of safety, engagement and comfort in the school environment. Sometimes it is a good idea to have a person who is trained to observe child behaviors, in this case the school guidance counselor or school psychologist, come in to the classroom to observe the child's classroom demeanor. Input from the counselor or psychologist can assist in creating an action plan to help your child, perhaps including a regular counseling component as an intervention.

If concerns persist or if you and the teacher cannot agree on the issues related to your child's social emotional well-being in the class, the next step would be to voice your concerns to the principal. The principal should listen to your concerns and then talk to the teacher. A meeting between the principal, you and the teacher may help to improve the classroom situation for your child.

In some cases you may find, and the principal may agree, that the teacher is not a good fit for your child. Teachers are human beings and like all human beings they have their strengths and weaknesses. If a particular teacher is not a good match for your child, a change of classroom might be a good choice, but this is also a choice that is fraught with possible negative consequences, including separating your child from already established classroom relationships. A classroom change must be taken with extreme caution, considering the pros and cons of such a move. It is not unusual for these issues to resolve themselves with time – some children have a difficult period of adjustment, but gain in comfort and engagement as the environment becomes more familiar, so any drastic measures must be taken cautiously.

What can I do if I suspect my child is being bullied in school?

Over the past ten to twenty years, state lawmakers and school leaders have placed a special emphasis on bullying in the schools. Awareness of bullying, programs to combat bullying, and classroom instruction aimed at raising awareness of bullying, are all prevalent in most schools today. All of this is well and good, but still bullying persists in schools, as it does whenever diverse human beings are gathered together in groups.

If you suspect your child is being bullied or if your child reports being bullied at school, you should take the following actions (adapted from *Steps to Take If Your Child Is Being Bullied*, published by the Pacer Center, a parent advocacy group.):[59]

Talk to your child –

- Acknowledge the behavior and help your child accept that this is bullying.
- Assure your child that the bullying is not his/her fault.
- Let your child know you are always there to support her/him.

- If your child comes to you with the information, praise him/her for telling you.

Ask specific questions –

- Who is doing the bullying?
- What happened?
- What kind of bullying was it? Verbal? Physical? Cyberbullying?
- When did the bullying happen?
- Where did the bullying happen?
- How long has this been going on?
- What did you do in response to the bullying?
- Keep a written record of your child's answers to these questions.

Talk about and practice possible ways to respond to the bullying with your child –

- If your child feels safe, s/he could try talking to the bully and saying firmly, "Leave me alone" or "Stop trying to bully me."
- Walk away from the bully, but do not run away.
- Identify an adult at school you are comfortable telling about the incident.
- Role play several scenarios and possible responses.

If the issues are not resolved by working with your child, then the next step to is to get the school involved.

Work with the school –

- Discuss the situation with your child's teacher/teachers and/or principal.
- Use the detailed report your child gave you to inform the teachers.
- Ask the teachers/principal what can be done at school to address the situation.
- Tell the teachers about what steps you have taken with your child.
- Discuss how the situation is impacting your child.
- Ask for a written copy of the school's anti-bullying policy.
- Keep a written record of what happens at this meeting.

If the issues are not resolved at the school level, you may want to proceed to the district level.

Work with the district –

- Write a letter or email to the district superintendent or anti-bullying coordinator requesting a meeting to discuss the situation.
- Prepare for the meeting by gathering all your notes from your discussion with your child and from your meeting with school officials.
- Take another person with you to the meeting as a note taker (and for moral support).
- Keep a written record of the meeting.
- Ask for a report from the administrator on what actions were taken and how well the district believes the issue has been resolved.

If the issues remain unresolved, you may want to consult a parent advocacy center like Pacer's National Bullying Prevention Center.[60]

No matter what the results of your efforts to intervene for your child in bullying situations, remember to keep your focus on the most important aspect of the entire process – the safety and well-being of your child. Your child should come away from the experience feeling empowered by the knowledge that his/her parents are supportive advocates and with strategies to employ when the next bullying incident occurs.

What resources will help me learn more about my child's social and emotional learning?

For books on the role of social and emotional learning in the home and the school try these:

Goleman, Daniel. (2005). *Emotional Intelligence: Why it Can Matter More than IQ*. NYC: Bantam Books.

Elias, M.J. and Arnold, H.A. (2007). *The Educator's Guide to Emotional Intelligence and Academic Achievement: Social-Emotional Learning in the Classroom*. Thousand Oaks, CA: Corwin.

For a website to learn more about the Responsive Classroom approach to social and emotional learning look here:

Responsive Classroom. https://www.responsiveclassroom.org/

For websites with great resources on the anti-bullying movement, including actions that children and parents can take to prevent and respond to bullying try these:

Pacer's National Anti-Bullying Prevention Center. http://www.pacer.org/bullying/

Operation Respect. http://www.operationrespect.org/parents/parents_overview.php

6

Technology and Learning

What is the role of technology in my child's learning?

In the classroom when we talk about technology, we talk for the most part about the use of computers in the learning environment. While computers offer the potential for many diverse and rewarding learning opportunities, it is important to remember that technology is only a tool for the teacher and for the learner. Like all tools for learning, computers are dependent on teachers for effectively planned lessons that use the power of computing to advance student learning in ways not available through paper, pencil and textbook. Schools often publicize their investment in technology (five computers in every classroom, two computer labs, an iPad for every member of the class), but none of this technological infrastructure is of much value unless it is used well, and it cannot be used well if teachers and schools cling to traditional modes of instruction.

Effective use of technology in schools means integrating the technology into the learning situation. Technology should be used to deepen and enrich the learning experience in four key ways: engagement, group work, interaction and feedback, and connection to real world experts. The use of technology should be as routine a part of student learning experiences as reading and taking notes. Technology has great potential to enhance student learning through a project based approach where groups of students work together to gather information, test a hypothesis, or solve a problem.[61] Ironically, this great and powerful personal tool is best used in schools as a part of group interaction that produces the best model for learning.

Technology provides almost instant access to the most current information available. This makes the computer a more useful and adaptable tool for learning than textbooks, that typically are only updated every 5 to 10 years. Computers also allow students to access information in a variety of ways, including through text, but also through video images and sound. Reluctant learners may find the many different avenues to learning available through technology more engaging and more in tune with their preferred learning styles.

Technology offers the opportunity for teachers to change from being a dispenser of information to a facilitator of learning. When technology is effectively integrated into learning, teachers not only fill the role of content expert, but also adviser and coach. Some of the best learning models take the teacher out from in front of the classroom and place them looking over the shoulder of the learner. Technology has the potential to enhance this learning relationship.

How can I know if my child's school is using technology well?

As we have seen above, just having technology in the school

does not improve your child's learning. Several factors, including how often technology is available to your child, how well the technology is integrated into instruction, and how well the technology resources are maintained, determine if technology is being used well in your school.

Here are some questions you can ask yourself to guide your inquiry into technology usage in your child's school. Many of these questions are suggested by Crystal Yednak in an article on the Great Schools website.[62]

- How much access does my child have to technology in the classroom?
- Does the school have a media lab and how often does my child have an opportunity to use it?
- What opportunities does my child have to learn about effective and safe computer use?
- Are computers and other technology aids up-to-date and in good repair?
- Does the school employ a technology expert who is responsible for the maintenance of the equipment?
- Is technology support readily available to teachers and students?
- Does the school have a reliable wireless network?
- Are specific projects planned that require students to use technology in their learning?
- Do students often work on group projects where technology is a key part of completing the work?
- Do teachers receive professional development aimed at the

effective use of technology n instruction?

- Do teachers use technology (Smartboards, Power Points, videos) effectively in their instruction?
- Do teachers use technology (email, classroom websites, social media) effectively for communication with parents and children?

What kind of technology should I have in the home to assist my child in learning?

When I was in elementary school I remember my parents going into hock to purchase a set of World Book encyclopedias for me to use for homework and projects. I loved these books and found them very useful – at least for a few years until the information in them became hopelessly dated. Today, parents who can afford it have the option to purchase a computer and an internet service and thereby provide their children with all manner of information and learning resources that are up-to-date.

The kind of computer you buy depends on the age of your child, your child's learning needs and what fits into your budget. One way computers have improved greatly over the last few years is in portability. It is likely sufficient for younger children to have a tablet type computer with a detachable keyboard for use in the home. Older students who have more written projects will likely want to have a laptop that combines a full-sized keyboard and reasonable portability. Good quality devices of this type are readily available now for under $500.

A stable internet connection is also important to allow children to access all the learning power that the World Wide Web can provide. Because of the emphasis on portability, an in-home Wi-Fi connection is advisable. With access to the internet comes very real worries about what kinds of material children can access. Most tablets and laptops now come with parental controls that allow you to monitor your child's computer use. Be sure to ask about the parental controls on a device before making any purchase. The independent non-profit organization, *Internet Matters,* has a website that is full of information about finding the right device to buy and providing for internet safety.[63]

Of course not everyone can afford computer devices and an internet connection. The Pew Research Center found that children from the lowest-income families are "four times more likely to be without broadband than their middle or upper income counterparts."[64] This creates a further barrier for poor children, a divide that has been called the "homework gap." In June of 2015, the Federal Communications Commission voted to grant 1.5 billion dollars to a program that will subsidize telephone services, and ultimately internet connectivity, for low-income families.[65] Whether this or other programs will work to narrow the homework gap remains to be seen.

In the meantime, it is incumbent on the school and school district to ensure that students are not disadvantaged by a lack of technology or connectivity in the home. Schools might do this by opening up computer labs in the school to families after school hours. One school district in southern California armed its school buses with Wi-Fi and parked the buses overnight in trailer parks where many low-income children lived, giving the children internet access.[66] Some community groups, like one led by Christopher Mitchell in Minneapolis, advocate for free community access to broadband services. Mitchell says, "Until we find a way to provide free Internet access, there's always going to be some measure of the population left behind; we have a long way to go to solving this problem."[67]

Beyond efforts to provide technology to families who cannot afford it, however, school districts must ensure that they provide alternative ways to complete assignments and to receive and send communications to the school that do not depend on technology. If individual projects requiring technology are assigned, alternative ways to complete the assignments must be provided for those who lack the necessary technological resources. If computer based group projects are assigned, schools need to provide time in school on school equipment for students to do the projects. If communication is conducted through email and websites, then equivalent print communication must also be provided. Parent groups can help in this effort by monitoring what is happening in the school, and by making sure that all school assignments and school communications are accessible to all students.

Is a cyber-school or blended learning school a good choice for my child's education?

A cyber-school, also called a virtual school, is a school that delivers its instruction entirely through online methods. Students enroll in the school, sign-up for classes and receive their instruction through curriculum that is delivered online. Contact with instructors is also online. Cyber-school teachers review student work and provide feedback entirely online. A blended school provides a combination of online instruction with some classroom instructional time. There are a variety of blended learning models, with some requiring more "face time" with teachers than others. Both cyber schools and blended learning schools are available to parents in many localities as "public" charter schools.

Cyber-school and blended learning advocates cite parental choice as one of the chief benefits of publicly supported online learning. Cost savings is another benefit cited by advocates. Since cyber-schools do not require any brick and mortar classrooms and because cyber-teachers typically are assigned many more students to oversee, costs are kept low. Other benefits that advocates see include the ability to personalize learning that may engage students more in content and the opportunity for children to learn in an environment free of the bullying, cliques and social distractions that may be present in schools.[68]

Detractors point out that while online schools may eliminate social distractions, they may increase online distractions. Without monitoring, students may be spending their instructional time playing video games or surfing the internet. Opponents also point to the isolated learning environment of the online school. Learning researchers have long established that learning is socially constructed; that is, we learn by interacting with others, including teachers and classmates, as we explore new ideas and integrate new knowledge.[69] Many educators worry that the social learning aspect of education will be severely limited in virtual schools, and that virtual chatrooms and message boards are a poor substitute for human interaction. Online learning also limits the interpersonal learning that comes from interacting with others in a classroom environment, those social and emotional aspects of learning that help children learn how to live and work in a diverse society.[70]

The biggest concern with cyber and blended learning schools, however, is that they have been shown to provide an inferior education. In a Center for Research on Education Outcomes (CREDO) study of virtual charters in Pennsylvania, a state with one of the largest cyber programs in the country, researchers found cyber-school students performed worse than students in brick and mortar public schools on tests of both reading and math.[71] The National Education Policy Center (NEPC) released a report that found similar deficiencies in the country's largest online education provider, K 12 Inc. One of the authors of the study, Gary Miron said:

> *Our findings are clear, children who enroll in a K12 Inc. cyber school, who receive full-time instruction in front of a computer instead of in a classroom with a live teacher and other students, are more likely to fall behind in reading and math. These children are also more likely to move between schools or leave school altogether – and the cyber school is less likely to meet federal education standards.*[72]

Most worryingly, a new CREDO study released in October 2015 found that:

> *Students who take classes over the Internet through online charter schools make dramatically less academic progress than their counterparts in traditional schools.*[73]

Technology unquestionably provides incredible possibilities for enhancing student learning, but the best approach is not to have technology provide direct instruction to students, but to open new opportunities for learning in school under the guidance of teachers and in cooperation with other students.

A cyber school or blended learning school may be the right choice for some children. Children who are having a hard time in the regular school, either because of social and emotional difficulties, lack of engagement in school, or health reasons, may find the online option a desirable alternative to classroom based learning. Parents need to weigh the options carefully and also consider the amount of time they wish to commit to their child's learning. Online learning requires consistent monitoring and lots of clarifying conversations with children. For most children a brick and mortar school that integrates technology thoughtfully into its learning design is the better option.

What resources can I consult to learn more about technology and learning?

For a book aimed at parents who are interested in looking at online and blended learning options try this:

Kanna, E. & Gillis, L. (2014). *Virtual Schooling: A Guide to Optimizing Your Child's Education.* NY: St. Martin's Press.

For a book aimed at teachers, but useful in helping parents understand how technology can be integrated into learning see this:

Whitaker, T., Zoul, J., & Casas, J. (2015). *What Connected Educators Do Differently.* Philadelphia, PA: Routledge.

For a book on blended learning also aimed at teachers from an education reformers perspective try this:

Horn, M. B., Staker, H. & Christensen, C.M. (2014). *Blended: Using Disruptive Innovation to Improve Schools.* San Francisco, CA: Jossey-Bass.

For a book aimed at helping parents provide a safe technological environment for their children try this:

Bush, N. & Goldstuck, A. (2014). *Tech-Savvy Parenting: A Guide to Raising Safe Children in a Digital World.* Johannesburg, S.A.: Bookstorm.

For a brief look at the pros and cons of the online learning alternative see this article:

Chen, G. (n.d.). Virtual Charter Schools: Pros and Cons of the Growing Trend. *Public School Review.* http://www.publicschoolreview.com/blog/virtual-charter-schools-pros-and-cons-of-the-growing-trend

For information on finding the right technology for your child's use in the home try this website:

Internet Matters. http://www.internetmatters.org/about-us/

7

Getting a Good Teacher in Every Classroom

What makes for a good teacher?

Google the question above and you will get thousands of hits. There is no shortage of opinion and no shortage of research on the topic. The answer to what makes a good teacher is, however, elusive. As University of Michigan professor, Jeffrey Mirel has said:

> *Teaching on the kindergarten through 12th grade level in the United States today is an incredibly challenging, complex and difficult enterprise.*[74]

A good teacher must be a skilled manager of a classroom filled with children from diverse backgrounds and with diverse needs. A good teacher must be knowledgeable in pedagogy, child development, and child psychology. A good elementary teacher must be conversant in a broad array of subject matter including literature, mathematics, social studies and science. A good secondary teacher must have deep knowledge of the content in a particular discipline and often multiple subjects within that discipline. A good teacher must be effective in oral and written communication with children and adults. A good teacher is skillful in using current technology and in helping students to use technology for learning.

But all of the intellectual skills enumerated above do not start to encompass all that we would want for our child's teacher. A good teacher must also be a passionate advocate for our children and a compassionate guide for our children when things don't go well. A good teacher celebrates our children's learning victories large and small, comforts our children when they are upset, corrects them when they misstep. No definition of teacher can be complete without this very human aspect, because the teacher is quite literally *in loco parentis* while our child is at school. All of us wish to know that our child is both cared for and taken care of by the teacher.

The complexity of the question of what makes a good teacher is made all the more complex because not all parents agree on what kind of teacher they want for their child. All parents are seeking a teacher who is a good match for their child. Some parents place high priority on a warm nurturing presence in the classroom. Other parents value a nurturing environment, but are more concerned with a teacher who provides a high level of academic challenge for their child. Still other parents want a teacher who runs a highly structured, no nonsense classroom because they believe that is the best learning environment for their child. So what one parent might perceive as a good teacher might not be perceived that way by another parent.

Ultimately, I think we must judge the quality of the teacher by asking these questions:

- Is my child learning the content of the class?
- Is my child learning skills for continued learning in the subject?

- Is my child developing a desire for further learning?
- Is my child engaged in the learning?
- Does the teacher provide for a balance between intellectual, social and emotional growth?
- Does my child enjoy the class?
- Does the teacher clearly communicate about the learning with my child and with me?
- Does the teacher seem to care about my child both as a student and as a person?

Teachers are professionals. As parents we have every right to insist that teachers meet professional standards. We should expect teachers to be knowledgeable, well-prepared, capable and highly engaged. As parents it is also helpful to understand that the teacher's job is a challenging one that demands meeting the needs of a diverse population of children by making hundreds of instructional, intellectual and social/emotional decisions every day.

How much does a good teacher matter?

Not surprisingly, a good teacher matters a great deal. Research indicates that the classroom teacher is the single most important in-school factor impacting learning. This seems to be a "no brainer". Teachers are the individuals best positioned to impact learning in the school. Much of the current corporate education agenda has been focused on teacher quality. It makes sense that if the teacher is the single most important in-school factor then we could improve schools by improving the quality of teachers.

Unfortunately, this focus on the teacher has led to a false narrative where teachers are blamed for the perceived educational woes of the nation. If we are falling behind in international tests, it must be the teacher's fault. If our children are not prepared for college, it must be the teacher's fault. The teaching profession has become the scapegoat for larger societal problems, some real and some imagined, that the country does not want to deal with seriously.

What is often de-emphasized in the narratives put forward by the education reformers is that, while the teacher is the most important in-school factor impacting learning, teacher impact pales next to the influence of family, neighborhood, and individual characteristics. Typically a teacher's impact is estimated to affect between about 10-20% of a child's learning, while all those factors beyond a teacher's control have four to five times more influence.

One of the things this means, of course, is that good teaching cannot, by itself, overcome the debilitating influence of poverty on a child's ability to learn. It also means that it may be very difficult to judge the effectiveness of a teacher without controlling for all the other outside of school factors that influence a child's ability to learn.

Education reformers like to say that out-of-school factors are beyond the influence of schools and teachers, so we must focus on the in-school factors in order to improve performance. Public education advocates point out that focusing on teachers will never move us far toward a long-term solution and that as a country, we must combine work to improve schools and schooling with an effort to alleviate economic inequity and improve the very conditions that have a far greater impact on a child's ability to learn.

Back in the 1950s, during the Cold War, when all Americans feared a nuclear attack from the Soviet Union, school children were taught to "duck and cover" in the school hallway during air raid drills. Of course, everyone knew that if a nuclear bomb fell in the vicinity of the school no amount of "duck and cover" training would save us. Focusing on teacher quality rather than focusing on income inequality is the "duck and cover" of the 21st century. We throw our hands over our heads at the real problem and instead of attacking poverty, we point a finger at the teachers.

How should a teacher be held accountable?

Since it is so difficult to define what makes a good teacher, it should be no surprise that the evaluation of teachers has long been a great challenge. The traditional model for evaluation of teachers has been to have the teacher observed by an administrator, usually the school principal, vice-principal or supervisor, and have that person pass judgment on the teacher's competence. Often newer teachers would be observed 3, 4, 5 times a year, while veteran teachers would be observed, generally, once a year. Virtually no one believed this system was adequate, but resources were rarely provided for a more rigorous approach.

The education reform movement, focused as it has been on the teacher as the major in-school factor for student success, seized on the general weakness in teacher evaluation and new research coming from economists to advocate for a value-added measures (VAMs) approach to teacher evaluation. This approach got the attention of many, including those in the U.S. Department of Education and the Gates Foundation, in part because it placed the value of a good teacher in economic terms, but also because it promised a comparatively simple way to measure a teacher's competence; a formula whereby a teacher's "value" could be mathematically determined using standardized test data and a statistical formula.

In a 2010 study, economist Erik Hanushek of the Hoover Institute at Stanford University posited that the difference of one standard deviation in teacher quality, as measured by student performance on standardized tests, could mean a difference in 400 thousand dollars in an individual student's earnings over a lifetime. He further stated that replacing the bottom performing 5-8% of teachers based on their value-added scores could move the U.S. near the top of international rankings in math and science.[75]

In 2011, another group of economists from Harvard and Columbia Universities published a large study that reaffirmed Hanushek's findings and supported a value-added model for assessing teacher competence.[76] VAMs primarily use student scores on standardized tests to determine teacher quality. They also use a variety of statistical measures to control for such variables as student background and family income. The authors argue that school districts should use VAMs in teacher evaluation, and remove the lowest performers as determined by these measures. Like Hanushek, they found that the difference between a high performing teacher and a lower performing teacher had a significant economic impact for the individual student and for the nation.

This research had all the stuff that makes for flashy headlines. The New York Times trumpeted that a "Big Study Links Good Teachers to Lasting Gain." In that article one of the authors, John Friedman argued that the message of the research is "to fire people sooner, rather than later."[77] Another author Raj Chetty affirmed, "of course there are going to be mistakes, teachers getting fired who don't deserve to be fired."[78] But the authors concluded that these value-added measures were worth the risk.[79] The long promised formula for holding teachers accountable had been discovered.

While education reformers embraced these economists' research, teachers, their unions and other researchers were skeptical. These critics focused on two main problems with the research: The difficulty of isolating all the factors that go into measuring a teacher's performance, and the large margin of error that these value added ratings create. Audrey Amrein-Beardsley, associate professor at Arizona State University, in a book length study entitled, *Rethinking Value Added Models of Education,* determined that these ratings were unreliable, invalid, nontransparent, unfair, and full of measurement errors, and were being used inappropriately to make key decisions about teacher retention and pay. She concludes:

> *[E]ducation policy makers and others cannot continue to address the supposed plight of America's schools by promoting and adopting an empirically and morally void accountability mechanism...based largely on false assumptions, myths, and overly simplistic fixes to highly complex problems.*[80]

Recently, the most comprehensive study of teacher evaluation ever attempted was conducted by the education reform minded Gates Foundation. In the three year study, 45 million dollars were spent to pin down the best way to evaluate a teacher and the results were published as the *Measures of Effective Teaching* (MET) in 2013.[81] The Gates Foundation claims to have figured out what makes a good teacher and how a teacher should be evaluated.[82] What did they find out? The MET study argues that teacher evaluation must take a three-pronged approach built on test scores, classroom observations done by multiple reviewers, and student surveys. The MET study argues that about one-third of a teacher's evaluation should be based on student standardized tests or "value-added" scores.[83]

While most education reformers praised the MET study and while many school districts were working to put the MET precepts in place, others were critical of the study. Value added opponents argued that placing one-third of a teacher's evaluation in the hands of unreliable, unstable statistical measures gave these measures too much power and would lead to teaching to the test, unhealthy instructional practices, and teachers refusing to teach the most difficult to teach children. Writing for the National Education Policy Center, researchers Jesse Rothstein and William J. Mathis concluded:

> *While the MET project has brought unprecedented vigor to teacher evaluation research, its results do not settle disagreements about what makes an effective teacher and offer little guidance about how to design real-world teacher evaluation systems.*[84]

Weighting value-added measures as 33% of the teacher's evaluation is also ill-advised. As the New Jersey based Educators for Quality Assessment of Teacher Effectiveness (EQuATE) put it in their report to Governor Chris Christie's Task Force on Teacher Evaluation:

> *Research studies show that the teacher's effect on value-added scores, based on [standardized] tests, accounts for only 3-4 percent of the variation. Fully 90 percent of the variation in VAMs is attributable to student characteristics and the interaction of learning/test-taking styles with the instruments used to measure achievement; it's not the teacher. To ascribe a weight to this measure that exceeds its explanatory power would be malpractice at best.*[85]

Lost in all of this is the chief purpose of teacher evaluation, which is to help a teacher continually improve performance. The chief argument against value-added measures is that they do little to help a teacher perform better at the job. Standardized test results provide the teacher with very limited knowledge about instruction or how to modify instruction. The information that these tests do provide is often delivered to the teacher after the students taking the tests have left that teacher's classroom, and even if that data were timely, it provides scant useful information. As suggested by the EQuATE report cited above, value-added measures should constitute about 3-4% of a teacher's evaluation, and even then, because these scores are so unreliable, should only be used as a check against more useful and substantive information.

The more useful and substantive information should come from classroom observations, actual student work samples, teacher self-reports, and student surveys. Observations should include full class length observations and briefer, more frequent drop-in observations. These observations should be done by qualified, certified observers, schooled in good instructional practices, who were exemplary teachers themselves before taking on a supervisory role. All observations, both full class length and brief drop-ins, should involve follow-up from the observer designed for teacher improvement.

Teachers should be asked to compile sample student work product including written assignments, projects, quizzes and tests, which can then be used to evaluate student learning growth over time. Since teachers improve their practice through self-reflection, a self-reflection document should also be provided as part of an evaluation process. Student surveys are another form of data that should be collected. Of course, student survey data can be tricky. While most students will likely give an honest appraisal to their teacher, some will be motivated by perceived slights or be angry at a teacher for holding him/her accountable for work or behavior. Surveys of younger students may also be unreliable reflections of teacher quality. However, when used appropriately as part of a conversation about student satisfaction in the classroom, student surveys can provide very useful feedback.[86]

Along with classroom observations, then, student work product, teacher self-reflection and student surveys are the components of an effective teacher evaluation/accountability program. They should form the basis for an ongoing conversation focused on instructional improvement and an end of year evaluative conference between supervisor and teacher.

Successful evaluation systems must be built on trust. Teachers do not trust the results of value-added measures for good reason – they have been shown to be unreliable, unfair and invalid. Trust is built through informed supervisors and reflective teachers holding professional conversations with each other around classroom practice and student performance. Once trust is established, the hard work of instructional improvement can begin.

Why do teachers have job protections like tenure and seniority?

For teachers in the public schools in grades kindergarten to 12, tenure is the contractual right of teachers to not have their jobs terminated without just cause. Most states have laws providing some form of tenure for teachers. Education reformers see tenure as one of the chief roadblocks to improving teacher performance in schools. They say that tenure laws make it difficult to get rid of bad teachers. While it is unclear who these bad teachers are (certainly the value added measures discussed above can't reliably identify them) and it is also unclear that firing teachers would improve educational performance,[87] tenure makes a convenient target for education reformers, because many in the public see tenure as unfair job protection.

In truth, tenure protections have been problematic, but not because tenure itself is bad or because too powerful unions have abused the due process rules. Tenure has become problematic because school administrators have been unable or unwilling to do the work necessary to remove a teacher by gathering the appropriate documentation and because the process itself has become filled with red tape, expensive litigation and lengthy delays. Problems of process do not make tenure laws wrongheaded, though. In fact, tenure is a necessary job protection for teachers.

The reason teachers need the protections of tenure are many. Tenure was first passed into law by state legislatures to protect teachers (mostly women of course) from being fired by local school boards for breeches of draconian rules like requiring them to be home by certain times, to be unmarried, to dress a certain way, to engage in only certain prescribed activities, etc. Tenure also protected experienced teachers from being fired in favor of a younger, cheaper teacher. Most importantly, however, tenure protects a teacher from being summarily fired for teaching unpopular ideas, for using innovative teaching methods, or for being a student advocate.

The Scopes "Monkey Trial" is perhaps the most famous case of a teacher being fired for teaching something unpopular. Teacher John Scopes was fired for teaching evolution in violation of Tennessee's Butler Act which forbade it. With evolution still a hot button issue in many communities, it is hardly a stretch to imagine that a teacher without the job protection of tenure could be fired for such an act today. And what of other controversial topics like climate change, reproductive rights, or even the origins of the Civil War? School is a good place to examine these issues, and if teachers are afraid to approach them because of the political climate in the community, the damage to education as preparation for citizenship would be devastating.

Some innovative teaching methods can be noisy and messy. Teachers attempting to provide their students with hands-on, real world activities often need to step out of the usual classroom construct to engage their students in learning. But because innovation often requires bending the rules of usual classroom decorum, some less enlightened administrators may find these efforts inappropriate. Without due process protections, teachers are more likely to stick to the standard instructional design and the students will be the losers.

Sometimes a teacher must be an advocate for a child, even when that advocacy flies in the face of the school's administration. For example, if a teacher, using his/her best professional judgment recommends that a child receive special education services, the school administration might object for a number of reasons, including lack of staff or cost. A teacher may also wish to argue against certain budget cuts, based on the professional judgment that the cuts would harm children. If a teacher's job is at risk for advocating for students in this way, these professional voices could be silenced and the children again would be the losers.[88]

So whether it is by providing the freedom to teach potentially controversial topics, the freedom to try innovative instructional practice or the freedom to advocate for children, tenure is a necessary component of creating the kind of schools we want.

Seniority means that in times of staff reductions due to declining school enrollment or budgetary crisis, the teachers with the least experience in the school are laid off first. Education reformers argue that this ties administrators' hands and that they may be required to keep an underperforming teacher, while releasing a higher, but less senior, performer. In my career as a school administrator in a district going through a budget crunch, I can tell you that this is true. It happened to me and I had the unfortunate task of telling some very good young teachers they were being laid off.

But as bad as the seniority system is, the alternatives are worse. If we do away with seniority, then in times of budget struggles, the most expensive, i.e., the most experienced teachers would be vulnerable. Secondly, experienced teachers are critical to the mentoring of new staff. If the new teacher coming into the building is seen as a potential replacement for your more expensive self, just how open will experienced teachers be to playing that critical mentoring role? We also need to ask what the future of education will be if young teachers moving into the profession know that each year they spend as a teacher is moving them closer to the axe because schools are chronically underfunded. Will potentially good new teachers be attracted to a profession where job security is subject to the budgetary whims of a state legislature and a local school board?

In sum, tenure and seniority are imperfect answers to complex problems. Certainly tenure protections should be carefully granted, administrators should do their due diligence in evaluating teachers, and when a teacher is documented as being a poor performer the removal process should be streamlined and less costly. And as my colleague, Peter Greene says, "Seniority sucks, but every alternative offered by [reformers] sucks more."[89]

How do we get rid of bad teachers?

But what about the bad teachers? An evaluation system built on trust and collaboration as suggested above may not sound like a way to rid the schools of bad teachers. If tenure and seniority are necessary for attracting and maintaining a good teaching staff, what do we do about all those bad teachers I keep hearing about?

Unquestionably, there are some bad teachers, just as unquestionably there are some bad doctors, some bad lawyers, some bad plumbers and some bad corporate CEOs. Education reformers base their narrative about bad teachers around standardized test scores. Teachers who raise children's scores are good, those who don't are bad. However, as we've discussed earlier and will look at again in Chapter 9, standardized tests are both a flawed and an unsatisfactorily narrow method for determining teacher quality. It is good to know that our children are learning in a particular teacher's class, but we are also interested in how well our children are developing socially and emotionally in the classroom. Probably most important of all we want to know that the teacher knows and cares about our child.

Using standardized test scores, which we know are highly correlated to student income levels, would lead us to believe that the bad teachers are concentrated in high poverty areas and all the good teachers are concentrated in wealthy areas. Teachers who work primarily with children with disabilities would also be more likely to be rated as bad teachers. This is clearly absurd and overly simplistic. Because teaching and learning is a complex process, identifying and removing ineffective teachers from the classroom must also be a complex process. Such processes have been tried with considerable success in several school districts throughout the country including in Toledo and Cincinnati, Ohio and Montgomery County, Maryland.

In Montgomery County, Maryland, the school administration, the teachers and the teacher union have worked together to develop the Peer Assistance and Review (PAR) teacher evaluation and development process. Under this negotiated agreement teachers are held accountable for the quality of their work, master teachers are employed to help teachers who are falling short to improve, and a panel of administrators and teachers are empowered to remove teachers who fail to meet established standards and who fail to improve after receiving peer help.[90]

The process is time consuming and costly, but effective. It is a good example of how teacher unions and administrators can work together for the common good. Teacher unions have no incentive to continue to carry ineffective teachers on their rolls. At the same time, teacher unions have a responsibility to their members, even those members who may be underperforming, to make sure they get due process under the law and under the employee's contract. The PAR system ensures this due process, and also ensures the public that those teachers who are not performing well will be removed from the classroom.

Of course, as with any human endeavor, the PAR process is not perfect, but it is light years better than any other teacher evaluation process I have seen. It has the benefits of involving both administrators and teachers in solving the problem, and it increases the probability that a good teacher will greet your child at the beginning of the school year.

For you as a parent, I would recommend that you investigate the evaluation process in the school district where you live to see if the administration and teachers are working together on teacher evaluation based on a model like PAR. One good thing about public schools is that as a parent, you have a voice in these decisions through public board meetings and the ballot box. This is a voice you likely will not have in a charter school or a private school.

How can my school or school district attract and retain good teachers?

Education reformers have suggested a number of ways to attract good teachers to work in challenging schools. Proposals have included incentive pay (providing a payment above the regular salary to sign up), merit pay (paying teachers who get better (test) results more), even providing prospective teachers with affordable housing near the school. These programs are likely to fail because they do not address what teachers are looking for most in a teaching position.

Teachers choose where they want to work, not based on financial incentives, but primarily based on working conditions. Teachers want to work in a clean, safe school that has all the resources and materials that will allow them to do their job well. Teachers want to work in a school that has a climate of collaboration and a spirit of teamwork. Teachers want to work in a building where they have supportive administrators who value their efforts and offer them informed, constructive criticism.

The federal and state obsession with data will actually exacerbate inequity in teacher distribution. If teacher evaluations are going to be based in some large measure on student standardized test scores, teachers are going to avoid school districts with high numbers of students in poverty. Teachers understand that standardized test scores for students living in poverty will be lower than affluent students' scores no matter how good the teacher is. They also understand that evaluation based in large part on student test performance is a highly invalid, unreliable way to evaluate their performance. Test-based accountability is simply unable to identify effective teachers and it labels as ineffective many, many fine teachers who do choose to work in high poverty areas.

Highly effective teachers also desire a high level of autonomy because they understand that the classroom teacher is best positioned to make instructional decisions about individual children. Inner city schools have responded to instructional challenges by becoming more and more prescriptive in their approaches to instruction. Highly effective teachers do not want to teach in a place where they are expected to be on the same page in the textbook as their colleagues on any given day.

Highly effective teachers have no interest in a school model based on merit pay. A reasonable living wage that considers their preparation and professional status is enough. Teachers recognize that the best schools to work in are collaborative, and that hare-brained ideas like merit pay destroy a collaborative climate. The corporate reformers' notion that competition is good in all things is simply wrong; it is particularly and specifically wrong in a profession like teaching.

Here is a checklist you can use to determine if your school district has the capacity to attract and maintain high quality teachers:

- Are the district schools clean, safe, well-maintained places to work?
- Are routine procedures clearly communicated and consistently followed?
- Is there a persistent tone of mutual respect between students and teachers?
- Are students actively engaged in the pursuit of knowledge?
- Are student discipline issues dealt with swiftly and fairly?
- Do the teachers appear to work collaboratively with each other?
- Do the administrators appear to work collaboratively with the teachers?
- Are there plenty of opportunities for teacher and administrator professional growth?
- Is teacher evaluation based on collaboration and focused on improvement?
- Does the district hire appropriately certified teachers?
- Are class sizes reasonable?
- Is the pay scale for teachers comparable to other area school

districts?

If you can check off all or most of the items on this list, your district will be able to attract and retain the best candidates for teaching positions. If you cannot, then you need to determine what the school district is doing to ensure that every school can meet these criteria, and then press them to set goals to meet these objectives.

What is Teach for America and how might it impact my school?

Teach for America (TFA) is a non-profit organization that was created to recruit recent college graduates, often from elite schools, to teach for two-years in low income communities. The idea was to eliminate "educational inequity" by making sure inner-city children had access to good teachers. The organization was founded by Princeton University student Wendy Kopp and has been embraced by the education reform movement.

Originally, TFA was intended to be a way of staffing positions that were left unfilled in urban areas. TFA was meant to fill gaps where teachers were hard to find. However, with the growth of charter schools and with the downturn in the economy in the 2000s, TFA has abandoned that mission and has become a major pipeline for staffing charter schools and for providing traditional public schools with cheap labor. Large charter operators like Lighthouse Academies partner with TFA to meet staffing needs. In fact, many charters will not expand in a region unless TFA has a presence there.[91] In Chicago in 2013, at the same time that the public school system was closing schools and laying off thousands of teachers, TFA was expanding its presence, essentially filling the positions of those teachers who had been laid off.[92]

There are two major problems presented by staffing a school with TFA recruits. The first problem is that TFA recruits are not certified teachers. TFA recruits earn their degrees in a variety of professional fields, but not in education. They receive a brief 5-week training session during the summer and then are thrown into some of the most challenging educational environments in the country. These recruits are well-meaning, most are very dedicated and most work hard. What they do not have is any professional credentials for teaching. They have not taught students in schools as college students who pursue a degree in education must do, and they have not done any course work in instruction, lesson planning, child development, classroom management, or any of the other key disciplines that education majors receive training in. TFA recruits, in other words, are not qualified to teach. There is a reason we have no "Surgeons for America" or "Lawyers for America". To be a doctor or lawyer you need a license to practice over and above the training you receive in a university degree program that affirms that you have met the state qualifications necessary to fill those roles. The same is true for teaching.

The second problem with TFA recruits is that they are, for the most part, not interested in a career in the classroom. College students who choose education for a major are typically committing themselves to a career in education. TFA recruits are committing to 2 years in the classroom. Some last a little longer, some not that long, but more than 85% are out of the inner city classroom after five years.[93] Even for the best trained teachers, it usually takes 3-4 years to get good at the job. At the point where TFA recruits might be getting good at the job, they are gone.

This high rate of TFA recruit turnover causes another problem. In order to become effective institutions of learning, schools need stability. They need stability in leadership and stability in staff. TFA creates an environment where instability is built in. Since TFA recruits only sign up for 2 years, the constant turnover of teaching staff creates disruption that works against the improvement of a school's educational program.[94]

TFA, which started as a good idea both focused on a need and devoted to social justice, has devolved into a multi-million-dollar enterprise aimed at undermining the teaching profession and remaking public education in the image of the corporate education reformers. If TFA recruits really wanted to help, they would volunteer as aides in inner city schools, work alongside professional teachers and, if they decided teaching was a career they wanted to pursue, go back to college and get properly credentialed.[95]

What can I do if I believe my child's teacher is not a good match for my child?

Just as there are all kinds of children and all kinds of parents, there are also all kinds of teachers. We can and should expect all teachers to be professional, knowledgeable in their field, communicative, and focused on the learning and well-being of children. We can also expect that different teachers will have different ways of accomplishing these responsibilities and different kinds of personalities when dealing with children. As parents, when conflicts or concerns arise, our jobs are to both listen to our children and to try to understand why the teacher is doing what s/he is doing.

Children should enjoy going to school, but school, of course, is not an unalloyed joy. Teachers have a responsibility to educate and sometimes that means requiring students to engage in learning tasks that are not fun for all. But if your child is not enjoying school in a general sense, appears unhappy or is reluctant to go to school, you should be concerned and you should be listening to your child. Sometimes a child will complain about the teacher. The teacher is unfair or the teacher yells a lot or the teacher doesn't call on me or the teacher doesn't explain things well.

In these situations, the first step is to talk to your child at length and try to pin down exactly what the child means. Probing questions will be helpful here. If the child reports, "The teacher is mean", you need to burrow into this generality to find out what your child means. You might ask "What does the teacher do that is mean?" If your child reports "The teacher picks on me" you will want to ask, "What did the teacher do that makes you say that?" or "What did you do before the teacher picked on you?" Kids often talk in generalities, so it is good to get as detailed a picture as possible of what is going on before taking any further steps.

If the concerns your child has voiced appear legitimate and are concerning to you, communicate to your child that you are his/her advocate and you will work with the teacher and others at the school to make sure school is a good experience. Begin your action by contacting the teacher. Make an appointment to discuss the matter, but do not try to have a conversation in the hallway or when picking your child up at school where attentions are divided. During the appointment ask questions that demonstrate your desire for clarity, and avoid an accusatory tone. Whenever possible, use your child's own words to describe the situation. You might begin with a statement like this, suggested by Susan Etheridge, associate professor of education at Smith College, "I'm coming to you with a problem I don't completely understand, but I'm hoping together we can best figure out [my child's] concern."[96]

Try to make it clear that you are not criticizing the teacher, but simply seeking clarification. Despite your best efforts, some teachers will respond defensively. Do your best to make it clear that you are just seeking to understand the situation. In the best case scenario, the teacher will see you as an ally, someone to work with to ensure a good working relationship with your child. In the worst case, you will feel frustrated with the teacher's response and feel that the issues have not been resolved. If the issues continue and subsequent meetings do not lead to resolution, then you may need to take the next step.

That step might be deciding to work with your child to help him/her deal with the issue. Kids don't have to like their teacher to learn, and sometimes the best thing for your child is to help with developing coping strategies. Kids do, after all, need to learn how to deal with different types of personalities.[97] But you may also decide that you would like to take the issue to the principal. In a meeting with the principal, continue to take the stance that you are seeking to work together with the school to make sure your child has the best possible experience. After this meeting, the principal may choose to speak to the teacher or ask you to meet with the teacher again with the principal in attendance. Either way, you will be looking for changes that make your child's experience better.

If change does not occur, as a last resort, you may want to ask the principal to change your child's teacher. Principals are very reluctant to do this, and parents should be reluctant to request it. A classroom is more than just a teacher; it is a little mini-society. Children establish relationships with their classmates that are often as important as those with the teacher. Parents must weigh the disruption to the child that changing the class would cause against the issues with the teacher. As Professor Etheridge suggests, it may be better for the child to stay put and "tough it out."[98]

Children deserve a well-prepared, informed, caring teacher. Teachers who fit this bill come in all shapes and sizes and with varying teaching styles and personalities. Parents need to serve the role of child advocate while also recognizing the challenges that teachers face, and with the awareness that dealing with different personalities is a critical part of the education their children need.

What resources can help me learn more about good teaching and good teachers?

For a brief summary of good teaching practices and poor teaching practices see here:

Characteristics of effective teachers. *Stanford Teaching Commons.* https://teachingcommons.stanford.edu/resources/teaching/planning-your-approach/characteristics-effective-teachers/

For more information on best practices in teacher evaluation read this report:

Hanover Research. (May, 2012). Best practices for including multiple measures in teacher evaluations. http://www.hanoverresearch.com/wp-content/uploads/2012/05/Best-Practices-for-Including-Multiple-Measures-in-Teacher-Evaluations-Membership.pdf

For ways that schools can attract and retain good teachers see these:

Farber, Katy. (2010). *Why teachers quit and what we might do about it.* Thousand Oaks, CA: Corwin.

ASCD. (May, 2002). Understanding and responding to the teacher shortage. *Infobrief.* Number 29. http://www.ascd.org/publications/newsletters/policy-priorities/may02/num29/toc.aspx

For the steps to follow when you have concerns with your child's teacher read this article:

Parenting.com. (n.d.). Five smart ways to handle teacher troubles. http://www.parenting.com/article/5-smart-ways-to-handle-teacher-troubles

8

The Common Core

What is the Common Core?

The Common Core State Standards (CCSS) is a set of learning guidelines in Mathematics and English/Language Arts (ELA) that outline goals for what children are supposed to know and be able to do by the end of each grade level from kindergarten through 12th grade. They were written during 2009 and 2010. According to the Common Core web site[99] the standards were created "to ensure that all students graduate from high school with the skills and knowledge necessary to succeed in college, career, and life, regardless of where they live." Forty-five states and the District of Columbia adopted the Common Core as their education standards, in part "encouraged" by the US Department of Education through Race to the Top.

Before the Common Core most states had established their own sets of learning standards. The federal government is expressly forbidden from mandating curriculum in schools, but the Department of Education used the power of stimulus money and a waiver from the impossible to reach goals of No Child Left Behind to convince states to adopt the standards. Alaska, Minnesota, Nebraska, Virginia and Texas never signed on to the Common Core, preferring to go with their own standards. More recently, as controversy has swirled around the Common Core standards, South Carolina and Oklahoma have repealed the standards and several other states have them under review.

Who created the Common Core State Standards (CCSS)?

According to the Common Core web site, the nation's governors and state superintendents of schools through their representative organizations the National Governor's Association and the Council of Chief State School Officers led the development of the standards. In reality the work of creating the standards was done by a small "working group" that consisted first of 24 people who set up a broad outline and then was expanded to 101 people for review. Both the work of these groups and the subsequent promotion of the Common Core were underwritten by more than 200 million dollars from The Bill and Melinda Gates Foundation. The Common Core standards were informed by the standards that were already in place in most states as well as standards used in other high performing countries.

The "lead writers" of the standards were David Coleman, Susan Pimentel and Jason Zimba. All three were members of the reform minded consultant organization, Student Achievement Partners (SAP). SAP is an education reform group also heavily funded by the Gates Foundation. Coleman is an education reformer and consultant who has been on the board of the Michelle Rhee led anti-teacher, anti-union organization, Students First. Susan Pimentel is a lawyer. Jason Zimba, who wrote the mathematics standards, is a mathematics and physics professor and long-time friend and business partner of David Coleman.

Of the 24 people on the core working group for the Common Core State Standards, only 8 had any K-12 classroom experience at all, and none was a current classroom teacher. At least 10 members of the group were closely affiliated with or employed by test development companies like Pearson, the Educational Testing Service (ETS) and the College Board. These included Laura McGiffert Slover, now CEO of the test development company PARCC (Partnership for Assessment of Readiness for College and Careers) who was on both the CCSS ELA and math work groups. The lead writer of the ELA standards, David Coleman, was appointed president of the College Board shortly after the adoption of the Common Core in the 43 states.[100]

In short, the Common Core State Standards were written by reform minded consultants, test company employees, college professors, and a few former teachers. Their work was reviewed by a larger group of 101 participants, again including consultants, test company employees, college professors, former teachers, and five people who were classroom teachers at the time of the review. No early childhood educators were involved in the writing of these K-12 standards.

Why do Common Core proponents say these standards are needed?

The development of the Common Core was driven by three factors: a desire for uniform standards across the country, the perceived need for students to be "college and career ready", and the performance of US students on international standardized tests of knowledge.

Prior to the Common Core adoption most states had their

own standards. According to Common Core proponents these standards varied in quality and rigor. The new standards sought to ensure that students in Mississippi would be held to the same standards as those in Minnesota. So, while this document is called the Common Core **State** Standards, the intention was for these to be national standards.

The authors of the Common Core were also concerned that many high school graduates were not "college and career ready". They determined this by looking at the number of remedial courses new college entrants were required to take, and through surveys of college administrators and instructors. The standards are intended to provide a structure that gets students ready to meet the reading and mathematics demands of college and the work place.

US students have typically performed in the middle of the pack on the Programme for International Assessment (PISA) exams, which measures student performance in reading, mathematics and science. Each time the PISA results are announced, newspaper and television headlines trumpet our lackluster showing. By including more "rigorous" standards from countries that do well on the PISA exams such as Finland and Singapore, the Common Core architects hoped to improve US student performance on these measures, which many people see as tied to our economic standing in the world in the future.

What makes the Common Core controversial?

Concerns about the Common Core began even before the final draft of the document was printed. Much of the early concern focused on the lack of transparency in the development of the standards. Traditionally, standard development at the state level was a public process that included committees of educators, content experts, parents, and business leaders, who created drafts, sent the drafts out for review, encouraged teachers to try them out with students and then revised the standards based on feedback. This was a process that took time, but one that also garnered broader based support.

In contrast, the process employed to develop the Common Core lacked transparency and was remarkably speedy. Speed can be a good thing, but because the Common Core was developed by a relatively small group of people, many of whom were testing experts and not teaching experts, and because there was no piloting of the draft standards, many teachers and school leaders were wary from the beginning. Even when the standards were opened to public comment, only a summary of those comments was released for public consideration.

Another early concern about the Common Core standards was that they flew in the face of well-established guidelines for developmentally appropriate practice and literacy instruction. In 2010 the Alliance for Childhood issued a statement signed by 500 early childhood experts expressing their "grave concerns" with the Common Core. The main concerns of these experts were that the Common Core would lead to long hours of inappropriate instruction in literacy and math for young children and the inappropriate use of standardized testing. Further, they stated there was no evidence that these standards would lead to later success for young children.[101]

Many literacy experts voiced concerns as well. Sandra Stotsky, professor of education reform at the University of Arkansas and a world renowned expert on standards development, has been sharply critical of the Common Core emphasis on reading more informational text and de-emphasizing the reading of literature. Stotsky believes the Common Core architects' obsession with students being "college and career ready" has driven them to a false conclusion about the place of literature in a K-12 curriculum. In an article titled *Common Core's Devastating Impact on Literature Study and Analytical Thinking* she says:

> *A diminished emphasis on literature in the secondary grades makes it unlikely that American students will study a meaningful range of culturally and historically significant literary works before graduation. It also prevents students from acquiring a rich understanding and use of the English language. Perhaps of greatest concern, it may lead to a decreased capacity for analytical thinking.*[102]

Literacy researchers have argued that the Common Core call for students to read more complex texts will disadvantage many readers, especially younger students, English language learners, and special needs children, and may actually help to widen the achievement gap the standards were supposed to address.[103] Many literacy experts have also noted that the Common Core emphasis on heavily text-focused study that deemphasizes the role of background knowledge in reading denies what 50 years of literacy research has taught us about the importance of students using background knowledge to help in comprehending the text.[104]

The Common Core curriculum in mathematics has also raised concerns for being confusing and developmentally inappropriate. The standards aim for a conceptual understanding of mathematics that goes beyond merely being able to get the right answer. The problem is that in practice, realizing this laudable goal has been very problematic. Teacher and writer Gary Rubinstein[105] has pointed out that the curriculum in use in New York State, EngageNY (also called Eureka Math) is riddled with confusing problems, errors, and boring lessons. Rubinstein and other writers, including award winning Long Island principal Carol Burris, have noted that the standards for younger children are often beyond their conceptual understanding.[106]

Other critics have pointed out that the Common Core authors communicate a contempt for teacher professionalism by emphasizing the centrality of textbooks in instruction,[107] or by touting instructional approaches that have been standard practice for decades as "innovations of the Common Core."[108]

Perhaps the most persistent criticism of the Common Core has come from educators and parents concerned with how closely the Common Core is tied to a new wave of standardized testing. The make-up of the working group chiefly responsible for writing the standards, which included more testing experts than classroom teachers, gives credence to this concern. From the start the standards were developed with testing in mind. In one way this is a good thing. Classroom teachers know that a good test can help them determine if their instruction has been successful. But when standards drive the tests, when the tests are far removed from the learning and the learners in the classroom, and when the tests have high stakes, many problems can and do arise. We will deal with the many problems of standardized tests in the next chapter. For now, suffice it to say that a major consequence of high stakes standardized testing is the narrowing of what gets taught in school. Common Core proponents like to say that the standards are merely guidelines, but when guidelines are tied to high stakes tests they become the curriculum.

A final concern that many have about the Common Core is that there is no mechanism for revision of the standards. Since the standards were put together so quickly and with so little piloting, we can assume that some of the standards will be problematic when put into action. Unfortunately, teachers who find a problem with one or more of the standards have nowhere to go for guidance or to ask for changes. States are permitted to change 15% of the standards to meet their local needs, but there is no process in place for revising the standards, and no review board to handle suggested changes.

Will the Common Core State Standards improve learning?

Not likely. Since the standards were not piloted before implementation, we can't know, but many leading educators believe that standards alone will not improve learning. One major concern is that the standards don't, and really can't, address the real reason for learning challenges in the country – poverty. When the performance of US students on international tests like PISA is controlled for poverty, our students score at or near the top. The fact is that the nearly 25% of American children who are living in poverty will trump any progress that might be achieved through any standards – good, bad or indifferent.

Even if we ignore poverty (which education reformers are wont to do), there is no evidence that standards will improve learning. A 2012 report authored by William Mathis of the University of Colorado, Boulder and published by the National Education Policy Center (NEPC) states flatly that: [109]

- *The adoption of a set of standards and assessments, by themselves, is unlikely to improve learning, increase test scores, or close the achievement gap.*
- *Children learn when they are provided with high-quality and equitable educational opportunities.*
- *Investing in ways that enhance these opportunities shows the greater promise for addressing the nation's education*

problems.

In a 2014 report for the Brookings Institution, Tom Loveless reviewed the progress in Common Core math to date and concluded:

> *The 2012 Brown Center Report predicted, based on empirical analysis of the effects of state standards that the CCSS will have little to no impact on student achievement. Supporters of the Common Core argue that strong, effective implementation of the standards will sweep away such skepticism by producing lasting, significant gains in student learning. So far, at least—and it is admittedly the early innings of a long ballgame—there are no signs of such an impressive accomplishment.*[110]

What will be the impact of the Common Core on my child's school?

As University of Oregon professor, Yong Zhao has pointed out in an article in *Education Week*, all medicine has its side effects. The Common Core is touted as a cure for low and variable standards in the states, but Zhao asks, "What are the side-effects of this proposed cure?"[111]

One thing we learned from No Child Left Behind is that standards tied to high stakes testing lead to a narrowing of curriculum. Since the Common Core both focuses on and tests only English/language arts and mathematics, we can expect that these areas will receive focus. Parents should watch their schools for the amount of time being devoted to science and social studies, but especially for reductions in the visual and performing arts and physical education. Are these valuable subjects being rendered second class citizens because of a focus on the Common Core?

Parents can also expect to see a flurry of activity around aligning curriculum to the Common Core. These curriculum changes come with costs ranging from paying teachers to write and review curriculum to purchasing new "Common Core aligned" textbooks and materials. Expenditures of this type in an age of very tight school budgets are likely to have side effects, including less money for class size reduction or non-Common Core related programs.

The Common Core implementation is having a profound impact on teachers and the teaching profession. Many teachers are concerned that the Common Core and allied testing will lead to teaching to the test, will stifle their own creativity as well as restrict their ability to develop creativity in children, and will force inappropriate instructional practices on them. Some teachers have reported being demoralized, and still others have decided to retire early or leave the profession.[112] The brain drain of experienced and accomplished teachers is likely an unintended, but clearly very real, consequence of the Common Core.

What will be the impact of the Common Core on my child?

Some schools, administrators and teachers have interpreted the Common Core call for rigor as meaning that kids need to be reading harder books and doing more challenging math at an earlier age. Since many have argued that the Common Core is not developmentally appropriate for younger children, such an interpretation could lead to some ill-advised changes in curriculum and instruction. Many speculate that early grades will become more rigid in their curriculum and learning expectations. The National Association for the Education of Young Children (NAEYC) has published guidelines for what kinds of teaching and learning should be happening in pre-school and primary grades.[113] Parents may want to consult these guidelines as Common Core changes come to their schools.

Parents of children at all ages should be on the lookout for practices that are detrimental to student growth in reading. A balanced literacy approach will observe the Goldilocks principal: some reading should be easy, some reading should be challenging, and some reading should be "just right". "Just right" reading provides students with some work to do to read and understand under the guidance of the teacher. A steady diet of very difficult reading does not make reading more rigorous, it just makes it hard. When reading is just hard, the will to read can be damaged. Children who don't enjoy reading rarely become proficient readers.

Parents will also want to be on the lookout for social and emotional impacts on their children. In April 2014, the comedian Louis CK rather famously tweeted about the negative impact of Common Core mathematics instruction on his children: "My kids used to love math. Now it makes them cry. Thanks standardized testing and common core!"-- Louis C.K. (@louisck).[114] It is unclear whether the fault here lies with the Common Core itself or with the implementation of it in Louis CK's children's school, but the end result is concerning. If the Common Core or its faulty implementation negatively impacts the joy of learning, no claims for the improved quality of the standards will hold much water.

What resources can help me learn more about the Common Core?

For a look at the standards and what the proponents say about them look here:

Common Core State Standards Official Website. http://www.corestandards.org/

Wiggins, G. (May 1, 2013). The Common Core Standards: A Defense. https://grantwiggins.wordpress.com/2013/05/01/the-common-core-standards-a-defense/

For a timeline of the development of the Common Core and a measure of the support of the Bill and Melinda Gates Foundation look here:

Cody, A. (2014). *The Educator and the Oligarch*. NY: Garn Press.

Editors. (n.d.). Pushing Common Core. *The Washington Post*. http://www.washingtonpost.com/wp-srv/special/national/gates-foundation/

Schneider, M. (August 27, 2013). A Brief Audit of Bill Gates Common Core Spending. *Deutsch29* blog. https://deutsch29.wordpress.com/2013/08/27/a-brief-audit-of-bill-gates-common-core-spending/

For critiques of the Common Core look here:

Cody, A. (November 6, 2013). Common Core Standards: Ten Colossal Errors. *Education Week*. http://blogs.edweek.org/teachers/living-in-dialogue/2013/11/common_core_standards_ten_colo.html

Loveless, T. (March 18, 2014). A Progress Report on the Common Core. *Brookings*. http://www.brookings.edu/research/reports/2014/03/18-common-core-loveless

Rubinstein, G. (May 9, 2015). You Reeka Math. *National Education Policy Center*. http://nepc.colorado.edu/blog/you-reeka-math

Walsh, R. (December 23, 2013). A Compilation of Common Core Concerns. *Russ on Reading* blog. http://russonreading.blogspot.com/2013/12/a-compilation-of-common-core-concerns.html

Yatvin, J. (February 27, 2012). A Flawed Approach to Reading in the Common Core Standards. *Education Week*.

http://www.edweek.org/ew/articles/2012/02/29/22yatvin.h31.html

Zhao, Y. (October 9, 2014) Common Core Side Effects. *Education Week.* http://blogs.edweek.org/edweek/finding_common_ground/2014/10/common_core_side_effects_worth_the_costs.html

For the impact of the Common Core on schools and teachers look here:

Effrem, K. R., MD. (May 27, 2013). The Effect of the Common Core Standards on Teachers and the Teaching Profession. *Education Liberty Watch.* http://edlibertywatch.org/2013/05/the-effect-of-the-common-core-standards-on-teachers-and-the-teaching-profession/

Thomas, P. L. (May 17, 2015). Power of Common Core Vocabulary Instruction Reaches Back to 1944. https://radicalscholarship.wordpress.com/2015/05/17/power-of-common-core-to-reshape-vocabulary-instruction-reaches-back-to-1944/

For the developmental appropriateness of the Common Core look here:

The National Association for Education of Young Children (NAEYC). http://www.naeyc.org/

Strauss, V. (November 9, 2013). Why young kids are struggling with Common Core math. *The Washington Post.* http://www.washingtonpost.com/blogs/answer-sheet/wp/2013/11/09/why-young-kids-are-struggling-with-common-core-math/

Walsh, R. (January 3, 2014). The Common Core Goes to Kindergarten. *Russ on Reading* blog. http://russonreading.blogspot.com/2014/01/the-common-core-goes-to-kindergarten.html

Walton, A. G. (October 23, 2014). The Science of The Common Core: Experts Weigh In On Its Developmental Appropriateness. *Forbes.* http://www.forbes.com/sites/alicegwalton/2014/10/23/the-science-of-the-common-core-experts-weigh-in-on-its-developmental-appropriateness/#72dbe5fa77cc

9

The Uses and Abuses of Standardized Tests

What are standardized tests?

According to the Glossary of Education Reform:

> *A **standardized test** is any form of test that (1) requires all test takers to answer the same questions, or a selection of questions from common bank of questions, in the same way, and that (2) is scored in a "standard" or consistent manner, which makes it possible to compare the relative performance of individual students or groups of students.*[115]

While many tests may be considered "standardized", we usually think of such tests as those being administered to large groups of students at the same time. Typically these tests use multiple choice questions as the primary question format, although true and false questions, short answer questions and essay questions are also used.

Standardized tests are used in this country for a variety of reasons, including their use as a measure of student achievement or scholastic aptitude. They are also used for college admissions testing (SAT, ACT), and international comparison tests (PISA). Another category of standardized tests are psychological tests such as IQ tests, that are often used to determine student learning abilities and disabilities, and are typically administered by a trained professional on an individual basis.

Standardized tests may be either **norm-referenced** or **criterion-referenced**. Norm-referenced tests measure the test-taker's performance against a normal or bell curve of other students' performance. In other words, an "average score" is determined through a statistical formula and then the test taker is measured against this average. Norm-referenced test scores are reported as a "standard score" based on the bell curve. So a student might be said to be at the 75th percentile, meaning that his/her score is better than 74 out of any 100 students who take the test. The SAT and the Terra Nova are prime examples of norm-referenced tests.

Criterion-referenced tests measure student performance based on some standard set of criteria. Almost all tests that are created by classroom teachers are criterion-referenced tests. A teacher teaches a certain set of information and then measures how much the student has learned through a quiz or test. But teacher made tests are not standardized tests. Criterion-referenced standardized tests seek to measure student achievement on a broad set of established standards. Currently for most states, this means tests that have been specifically developed to measure student achievement as defined by the Common Core State Standards (CCSS).

Common Core aligned tests have been created by two different testing companies, Pearson (PARCC test) and Smarter Balanced (SBAC). Some states have opted to develop their own assessments, but these tests have tended to be very similar to the PARCC and

SBAC.

Here is the breakdown of tests by states:

PARCC: Arkansas, Colorado, District of Columbia, Illinois, Louisiana, Maryland, Massachusetts, Mississippi, New Jersey, New Mexico, Ohio, and Rhode Island.

SBAC: California, Connecticut, Delaware, Hawaii, Idaho, Iowa, Maine, Michigan, Missouri, Montana, Nevada, New Hampshire, North Carolina, North Dakota, Oregon, South Dakota, Vermont, Washington, West Virginia, Wisconsin, Wyoming.

As of this writing, other states are developing their own tests, but we can expect, as has been the case in New York, that they will be similar to PARCC and SBAC because they are being built on similar criteria.

What makes standardized tests controversial?

Standardized tests have been a fact of public school life in the United States for 100 years. Chances are if you went to public school, you have taken your share of these tests. Schools have traditionally used the tests to assess the effectiveness of school-wide programs, to make curricular adjustments, as a shorthand way to inform parents about their child's progress as measured against national norms, for individual student placement, and to determine college aptitude. In the past these tests, other than perhaps the SAT, got little publicity and generally took up a small amount of time in the total school year. While some complained that standardized tests were often culturally biased, were a better measure of parent income than student achievement, and not very useful for making judgments about individual students, the tests flew under the radar because they had limited impact on schools, students, parents or teachers.

All this changed with the passage of No Child Left Behind in 2001. Suddenly standardized testing had become a very high stakes game. Where previously tests were given about three times in the 12 year career of the child at school, now students would be tested every year from grades 3-8 and again in grade 11. Schools would be judged as "failing" based on their test scores. Teachers and administrators could be fired and schools could be closed based on the results of standardized tests. Many states passed laws that made it mandatory to retain 3rd graders who failed to pass a standardized reading test. Then in 2010, Race to the Top tied teacher evaluation to student performance on standardized tests. Suddenly, a school's existence, a teacher's job, and a child's future were being closely tied to scores on standardized tests.

When these tests became a high stakes game for all involved, they became very controversial indeed. Researchers, teacher unions, education reformers, parents, pundits, news organizations and students all began to weigh in on the issue. Clearly, with so much at stake, it was necessary to look closely at standardized tests to see if they could hold up to close scrutiny. Could these tests be used appropriately for the purposes that education reformers wanted?

What are the limits of what standardized tests can measure?

Standardized tests, like most tests, can be useful in providing information about performance at the individual, classroom, school, district, state, national, and even international level. There are many problems with these tests; however, that make their use problematic for high stakes decision making. The organization Fair Test has identified a number of these problems:[116]

- Standardized tests can measure only a small subset of

student knowledge and abilities, and typically only a small subset of the actual standards being measured.

- Standardized tests have difficulty measuring important higher level thinking skills like the ability to analyze, evaluate, and be creative.

- The lengthy turnaround time for scoring most standardized tests makes them nearly useless as a diagnostic tool for individual children. Often the test results are not available until a student has moved on to the next grade.

- Since a standardized test offers only a snapshot of student performance it is not helpful in determining why the student might be struggling or how instruction needs to be changed to meet the student's needs.

- The results of standardized tests can only be used to suggest student strengths and weaknesses; a variety of measures are needed to get a full picture of a learner.

- Well-designed classroom assessments can provide richer understandings of student performance and a better guide for instructional changes.

The one thing that standardized tests are able to consistently measure accurately is the income of the parents of the children taking the test.[117] Over many years we have seen that the more affluent the parents in a school district, the higher the performance of children on standardized tests. Here is how education journalist, Alfie Kohn, puts it:

> *Don't let anyone tell you that standardized tests are not accurate measures. The truth of the matter is they offer a remarkably precise method for gauging the size of the houses near the school where the test was*

administered. Every empirical investigation of this question has found that socioeconomic status (SES) in all its particulars accounts for an overwhelming proportion of the variance in test scores when different schools, towns, or states are compared.[118]

In an era of high stakes testing, this means that schools in high poverty areas are certain to score lower than wealthier districts, schools in high poverty areas will be more likely to be labeled as "failing", and teachers working in high poverty areas are more likely to get poor evaluations.

What impact does a focus on standardized testing have on a school program?

According to Fair Test, when standardized tests are attached to high stakes, like student promotion and placement or teacher job security and school failure, they have the effect of narrowing the curriculum and driving teachers to use large amounts of class time on test preparation.[119] The PARCC and SBAC tests, as well as other Common Core based tests, measure performance on reading, writing and math only. This can mean, and in many schools already has meant, that less time is devoted to social studies, science, music, art and physical education.

The focus on test based accountability has driven many schools to do away with recess in elementary schools. Many new elementary schools are being built without playgrounds. When money is tight, as is almost always the case, schools need to make hard decisions about whether to cut arts or athletics programs in order to focus the limited available money on tested subjects.

Ultimately, this narrowing of the school program offerings will hurt children. A public school must offer a well-rounded program that includes the arts, the social sciences, and health and physical education. Children have many paths to learning, and many paths to becoming a well-rounded person. Arts and physical education programs are vital to maintaining many children's engagement in school. When high stakes tests limit the programs that schools can offer, all kids suffer.

With their job on the line or the academic reputation of their school under scrutiny based on standardized test scores, we can expect that teachers and administrators will give those tests a prominence in the instructional program that is not warranted. Many schools have responded by devoting large chunks of instructional time to test preparation.[120] In some schools this has even worked. Long hours of test preparation have led to improved test scores, especially in math where scores seem to be more impacted by test preparation than in reading and writing.

The problem is, of course, that when long hours are spent on test preparation, other more important instructional priorities are lost. As Kevin Welner and William Mathis of the National Education Policy Center (NEPC) have said, test based accountability in public education has meant: [121]

- Making schooling less engaging and creative.
- De-professionalizing teachers and teaching.
- Abandoning our past pursuit of learning that fully encompasses arts, music, social studies, and science.
- Marginalizing values and skills that help students develop the ability to cooperate, solve problems, reason, make sound judgments, and function effectively as democratic citizens.

If education is preparation for a college, career and a life well-led, then test preparation and standardized testing should not drive what is happening in schools, but should occupy only a small corner of the instructional program.

What does the standardized test score tell me about my child?

A good standardized test can give you a rough approximation of where your child stands compared to others in the school, the school district, the state, and the country. The current trend toward tests based on the Common Core State Standards, or something similar, will purport to show you how well your child is doing in achieving those standards. Whether these tests will be reliable and valid measures of this remains an open question at this writing.

It is important to understand that your child's performance on the test is at best a quick, fuzzy snapshot of all your child knows and is able to do. Standardized test performance, high, average or low, should always be considered in the context of your child's day to day performance in school. Report card grades may or may not be aligned with standardized test performance, because they consider many factors (critical thinking, attitude, homework completion, behavior, etc.) not measured by standardized tests.

The best information about your child's progress can be provided by the classroom teacher who is working with your child everyday. You will want to ask to see samples of your child's classwork and ask your child's teacher how s/he views the test scores in the light of your child's daily performance. If your child's test scores are low, but grades are high, the classroom teacher should be asked about this. Decisions about learning support, gifted placement or tutoring, and certainly retention should be made in conjunction with the teacher and not based solely on a standardized test score.

What can standardized tests tell me about my child's school?

A good standardized test can give you a rough approximation of how your child's school performs as compared to other schools in the district, in the state, and in the country. Again, the test provides only a very limited profile of the school, generally focused on just a few subjects (in the case of Common Core aligned tests only math and language arts) that are not reflective of the quality of the educational program as a whole.

It is important to remember that differences between schools and between school districts in standardized test performance will be greatly influenced by the socio-economic status of the children attending the school. Even within a school district we would predict that schools with a higher percentage of children living at or near the poverty line (usually measured by the percentage of children receiving free or reduced lunch) will produce lower overall test scores. This is clearly not an indictment of the school, but of economic and social inequity.

What do standardized test scores tell me about my child's teacher?

Not much. Despite the requirement in Race to the Top that teacher performance evaluation be tied in some way to student standardized test scores, study after study has shown that the statistical measures used to determine the impact a teacher has on student test scores, called "value-added measures" or VAMs, are volatile and unreliable. The leading organization of professional statisticians in the country, the American Statistical Association, has declared VAMs to have very limited usefulness in judging the performance of individual teachers, and suggests they are best used, just as all standardized test scores have been used in the past, to inform school and district performance.[122]

The reason that standardized tests are poor indicators of teacher quality are many. First, students are not assigned to teachers randomly, so in any given year a teacher might get a group of students who are struggling to master reading, writing and math. Principals often assign students to teachers because they view the placement to be a "good fit." Teachers who have a reputation for providing a highly nurturing envioronment may find they are assigned a high proportion of students who lack self-confidence, whereas teachers who have a reputation for providing a very structured environment may find they are assigned students who have been identified as needing lots of structure.

Even if students could be assigned randomly, standardized tests cannot account for the influence of all the other teachers the student has had in prior years and during the current year. All teachers build on the work of the teachers before them. Finally, as has been discussed earlier, standardized tests do not account for the kind of home and neighborhood the student lives in, which has a far greater impact on student learning (and test scores) than any teacher based factors.

How should I talk to my child about taking standardized tests?

For most children taking a test is a cause for some mild anxiety. Research has shown that a little bit of test anxiety is a good thing.[123] A small amount of concern can help children work hard, focus, and do their best work on any test. A large amount of anxiety, however, can cause a child to be unable to focus or to access the knowledge needed to score well on a test.

When the test is a big, long standardized test that the children have been hearing about all year in school, of course, the potential for high levels of anxiety are present. When talking to your child about these tests, the best approach is to encourage "doing your best work" and "giving your best effort", but not over-empahsizing the test's importance. Remember no matter how high the stakes, these tests are at best a snapshot of performance on a narrow subset of student knowledge and abilities taken at one moment in time. So, kids should understand that while it is important to do their best work, it is not important enough to lose sleep over. In fact, a good night's sleep is important to doing their best.

Sometimes we can communicate to our children that the tests are very important in subtle ways we do not even realize. High scores on these tests should not be celebrated with monetary rewards or gifts and low scores should not be punished. Effort over time should be rewarded, good deeds should be rewarded, but rewarding tests scores gives these tests a prominence they do not deserve and may increase a child's anxiety about the tests.

Should I be concerned with how my child's test performance data is shared in school and beyond?

In a word, yes.

One strategy that education reformers have adopted and encouraged is the "data wall." A data wall is a chart that shows students names (or student ID numbers) and those students' scores on standardized tests, often color coded to show levels of performance from high to low. When these data walls are used as guidance for teacher planning and differentiation of instruction, and when they are kept out of sight of all except those teachers, they can be an effective practice. When this data is hung in the hallway of the school for all to see, as has become the practice in many schools, it is quite simply child abuse.

This public type of data sharing is supposed to act as a motivator for children. To my mind, and to the minds of many educators, this practice is not only a poor motivational strategy, but an unconsionable abuse of power by school officials.[124] In fact this "motivational strategy" may violate federal law under the Family Educational Rights and Privacy Act (FERPA). Generally, schools must have written permission from a parent to release information from a student's educational record.

If your child's school puts your child's "data" on public display, I recommend that you ask that your child's name or ID be removed immediately. I also suggest that you request that the school reconsider the policy and take down the wall. Finally, if you do not get satisfaction consider filing a FERPA complaint.

Your child's data may be shared in other ways that you should be aware of. The Gates Foundation, which financed the creation and promotion of the Common Core, spent an additional $100 million on a data collection product called InBloom. According to Leonie Haimson of Student Privacy Matters, InBloom was designed to collect all kinds of student data, analyze it and provide it to vendors who would create learning tools to meet student needs.[125]

InBloom was collecting student and parent names, grades, test scores, detailed disciplinary and attendance records, health records, disability status, race/ethnicity, immigration status, and arrest records. The data was to be stored on a cloud operated by Amazon.com and designed by Amplify, a company owned by media mogul Rupert Murdoch.

Fortunately, parent protests, led by Haimson, revealed what InBloom was up to and the states and school districts that had agreed to participate pulled out. InBloom closed up shop in spring 2014. Threats to student privacy still exist, however. Twice in the last 10 years FERPA laws have been weakened to allow more sharing of student data to "authorized representatives", who were defined as any outside party that the school chose to authorize, whether they were under the control of the school or not. There are also questions about the security of storing student data on "clouds", which have been shown in many recent incidents to be vulnerable to hacking.

In this data climate, the best advice for a concerned parent is to be diligent about how your child's data is being gathered and shared, and to question any school action that may make sensitive information available to commercial interests. The watchdog organization School Privacy Matters has developed a useful set of guidelines for privacy laws: [126]

1. **Transparency** – Parents must be notified in advance when disclosure of any student data to persons or entities outside the school or school district is planned.

2. **No commercial uses** – Sharing of student data for commercial or marketing purposes should be banned.

3. **Security protections** – At a minimum student data should be encrypted and password protected.

4. **Parental/Student rights** – Parental consent must be obtained for any sharing of data. Parents have the right to remove errors.

5. **Enforcement** – Fines and sanctions for failing to follow the law.

Until such a law is passed in your state, trying to ensure that your local school or district abides by the first four principles will help to provide a measure of assurance that your child's data is not up for grabs by anyone.

If high stakes standardized tests are poor measures of student knowledge, teacher effectiveness and school performance, what are the alternatives?

Tests are central to instruction. It is the test that determines what is taught. If the test is a standardized test, then what is taught will not be very rich and varied. Education theorist, critic and consultant Grant Wiggins says that "a genuine test of intellectual achievement doesn't merely check standardized work in a mechanical way."[127] Wiggins calls for "authentic assessment" that measures what we truly want students to know and be able to do. In other words if we want students to show that they know how an electrical circuit works, we need to give them a test where they construct a successful electrical circuit. If we want students to be able to read, analyze and discuss a short story, we should ask them to read, analyze and write or talk about the story.

Authentic assessment is closely tied to instruction. An assessment should not only inform the teacher about student achievement, but also inform the student about what s/he knows and does not know.[128] Obviously, this type of assessment takes time, money and a high level of professional judgment. Standardized tests in the long run would probably be cheaper and faster, and would remove the messy human factor of judgement from the equation. They would also yield much less reliable and actionable data, and do precious little to inform the teacher or the student about next steps.

I had the opportunity to participate in a state wide attempt at authentic assessment in the late '90s. The New Jersey Department of Education developed, with input from teachers, parents and community members, a rubric for assessing student performance in public speaking. In the spring, students were given the task of preparing a short speech on a topic that was provided for them, and then presenting the speech to a team of evaluators.

Evaluators scored the speech, conferred, and gave the student a proficiency score and a copy of the rubric to show strengths, weaknesses, and suggestions for improvement. In this way, the student's learning was documented and feedback was immediately available for the student for continued learning, and also to the teacher for planning future instruction. Authentic assessment happens at the juncture of teaching, learning and performance, and therefore provides a clearer picture of achievement.

A series of authentic assessments for each student could be gathered in a portfolio. Just as an artist, photographer or actor prepares a portfolio of work to show to prospective employers or clients, so too can a student, with the guidance of the teacher, prepare a portfolio of work that reveals learning accoplishments throughout the year. This portfolio documentation provides a much richer picture of the student's learning for the teacher, the student, and the parents.

A teacher's evaluation, too, could best be accomplished through the portfolio. A teacher's portfolio might contain sample lesson plans, samples of student work, samples of assessments given to students, copies of observations, documentation of student learning, documentation of improved practice based on feedback from observations, documentation of professional development, samples of parent communication, and more. As with a student portfolio, the teacher portfolio gives a richer, more complete picture of the performance of the teacher than any standardized test could provide.

Finally, a school's performance could also be best thought of as a portfolio providing evidence of meeting student's needs. The school's portfolio would include standardized test scores, but would also include reports on programs, evidence of a rich and varied curriculum, documentation of meeting the needs of all children, documentation of efforts to invite parent participation in the life of the school, reports on hiring and evaluation processes, and much more.

Authentic assessments are time consuming and are influenced by human factors that statistics cannot always control for. They are also much more valuable as tools for guiding decision making and for informing the public than are the quick, fuzzy snapshots provided by standardized tests.

What resources can help me learn more about standardized tests?

If you only read one book on the impact of standardized testing on education, read this excellent account comparing China's test driven school system with that of the United States:

Zhao, Yong. (2014). *Who's Afraid of the Big Bad Dragon: Why China Has the Best (and Worst) Education System in the World.* Hoboken, NJ: Jossey-Bass.

Another excellent book length treatment of the standardized test controversy can be found here:

Harris, P., Smith, B.M. and Harris, J. (2011). *The Myths of Standardized Tests: Why They Don't Tell You What You Think They Do.* New York: Lanham, MD: Rowman and Littlefield.

For the history of how the current focus on testing became a

national priority read this:

Kuhn, J. (2014). *Test and Punish.* Pacific Grove, CA: Park Place Publications.

For a primer on standardized testing aimed at parents see here:

Public Broadcasting System. (2014). Testing our schools. *Frontline.* http://www.pbs.org/wgbh/pages/frontline/shows/schools/etc/guide.html

For an article length defense of yearly standardized testing see here:

Hyslop, A. (January 9, 2015). Five reasons getting rid of annual testing is a dumb idea. *Education Post.* http://educationpost.org/5-reasons-getting-rid-annual-testing-dumb-idea/#.VZZt-1vlViko

For more on data walls see here:

Strauss, V. (February 14, 2014). How data walls in schools can humiliate kids. *The Washington Post.* http://www.washington-post.com/blogs/answer-sheet/wp/2014/02/14/how-data-walls-in-classrooms-can-humiliate-young-kids/

For more on the relationship between wealth and standardized test scores see here:

Zumbrun, J. (October 7, 2014) SAT scores and income inequality: How wealthier kids score higher. *Wall Street Journal.* http://blogs.wsj.com/economics/2014/10/07/sat-scores-and-income-inequality-how-wealthier-kids-rank-higher/

For more on the consequences of high stakes standardized tests see here:

Editors. (December 17, 2007). Dangerous consequences of standardized tests. *Fair Test.* http://www.fairtest.org/dangerous-consequences-highstakes-standardized-tes

Strauss, V. (February 13, 2015). No Child Left Behind test based policies failed: Will congress keep them anyway? *The Washington Post.* http://www.washingtonpost.com/blogs/answer-sheet/wp/2015/02/13/no-child-left-behinds-test-based-policies-failed-will-congress-keep-them-anyway/

For more on student test anxiety see here:

Hall-Flavin, D.K. (2014). Is it possible to overcome test anxiety? *The Mayo Clinic.* http://www.mayoclinic.org/diseases-conditions/generalized-anxiety-disorder/expert-answers/test-anxiety/faq-20058195

For more on the use of standardized test scores to measure teacher quality see here:

Editors. (2014). ASA statement on using value-added models for education assessment. *American Statistical Association.* https://www.amstat.org/policy/pdfs/ASA_VAM_Statement.pdf

Baker, B. (April 19, 2012). The toxic trifecta, bad measurement & evolving teacher evaluation policies. *School Finance 101.* https://schoolfinance101.wordpress.com/2012/04/19/the-toxic-trifecta-bad-measurement-evolving-teacher-evaluation-policies/

For more on student data privacy issues see here:

Administrator. (June 22, 2015). Five principals to protect student data privacy. *School Privacy Matters.* http://www.studentprivacymatters.org/five-principles-to-protect-student-data-privacy/

For more on authentic assessment see here:

Wiggins, G. (April, 2011). A true test: Toward more authentic and equitable assessment. *The Kappan*, V92 N7. http://www.nisdtx.org/cms/lib/TX21000351/Centricity/Domain/21/j%20 carlisle/ATrueTest_Wiggins.pdf

10

The Standardized Test Opt Out Movement

What is the opt out movement?

The opt out movement is a grass roots civil disobedience movement designed to protest the overuse and misuse of standardized testing in evaluating students, teachers, and schools by simply refusing to take the test. For the most part, this opt out movement is aimed at the new set of standardized tests developed to align with the Common Core: the PARCC and the SBAC tests and similar tests in other states.

It is an effort that is growing rapidly into a national movement. In 2014 there were opt out movements in about half of the states. In 2015 there were opt out movements in all 50 states. In New York State alone, more than 200,000 students opted out of some form of the Common Core aligned tests in 2015. This represented more than 15% of all school students in the state.[129]

One measure of the growth of the opt out movement is the amount of media coverage it has been receiving. The movement has been the topic of multiple articles in the New York Times, the Washington Post, Newsweek, the Huntington Post, U.S. News and World Report, and reports on NPR, CNN and many others. Opt out is a hot topic and the movement has gotten the attention of critics and advocates of yearly testing.

Another measure of the growth of the movement is that the organization United Opt Out National held its first ever national conference in Ft. Lauderdale, Florida in 2015. The second annual conference will be held in Philadelphia in February 2016. Speakers at the conference will include professor of linguistics and testing critic, Stephen Krashen, author and former NPR and New York Times journalist, Chris Hedges, and long-time social and civic activist, Bill Ayres. Attendees will discuss topics like community empowerment, student activism, and organizing for opting out.

According to Monty Neill of the testing watchdog organization Fair Test, the movement is growing because increasing numbers of parents are concerned that there is too much testing going on and that much of it is not helpful in improving education. As Neill put it:

> *There've been a number of surveys in states as well as national surveys that are showing (frustration with testing) as a reaction among parents and the public generally, so there's a sense that this testing has just gone round the bend.*[130]

Who is behind the opt out movement?

Corporate education reform advocates argue that the opt out movement is largely led by teacher unions, but the facts reveal a more complex picture. The opt out movement began on many fronts, beginning with a loose coalition of educators and parents and growing to include more organized parent groups like Save Our

Schools and United Opt Out. The teacher union leadership actually resisted the opt out movement for years, until forced to get on board by the growing concerns voiced by rank and file members.

Opt out protests can take many forms: student led, teacher led, and parent led. At Nathan Hale High School in Seattle, the 11th grade class as a whole decided to opt out of the test and simply did not show up on the days the test was administered. At Princeton High School in New Jersey, more than 70% of high school students opted out of the tests they were scheduled to take.

Sometimes it was teachers who refused to give the test. Teachers in Colorado, Washington and Florida have publicly announced that they were opting out of administering the test primarily because they felt the tests limited their ability to teach children well and meet individual needs, and because they saw the tests as harmful to the entire enterprise of public education. As one teacher and literacy coach, Peggy Robertson explained:

> *I take objection to the fact that our children are being used as guinea pigs* in *an experiment to implement standards which were never field tested, are copyrighted, were not created using a democratic process, and were not created with the serious input of classroom teachers.*[131]

In Seattle, Washington, teacher Jesse Hagopian led a boycott of another standardized test, the Measures of Academic Progress (MAP). Hagopian and all of the teachers at Garfield High School refused to administer the MAP saying it was not valid, not aligned with the curriculum and used up too much valuable instructional time.[132]

For the most part, however, the opt out movement has been a matter of parents choosing to not allow their children to take the test. According to Frederick M. Hess, director of education policy for the American Enterprise Institute, 68% of parents don't believe standardized tests help teachers teach and only 31% think it is a good idea to use standardized tests to evaluate teacher performance.[133] Parents have come to realize that these standardized tests do more harm than good for kids. Some of these parents have decided to opt out of the tests.

The parent movement was particularly strong on Long Island, NY, where 65,000 students, or almost 45% of school children in grades 3-8, opted out of the test. Parent Deborah Brooks was quoted in Newsday, the newspaper of record on Long Island, as saying:[134]

> *I would hope that the reasons the majority of parents are doing it are the reasons this whole movement started. And that is to say that these tests are not valid.*

Parent Jeanette Deutermann was quoted in the same article as saying:

> *Our message is finally starting to make an impact. This is no longer just some noise being made. This is a true stance, and we are going to change the way they are using testing in New York State.*

How have education reform advocates responded to the opt out movement?

For the most part education reformers have viewed the opt out movement with disdain. U. S. Secretary of Education, Arne Duncan, rather famously said that the protests were being led by:

> *... white suburban moms who – all of a sudden – their*

child isn't as brilliant as they thought they were and their school isn't quite as good as they thought they were, and that's pretty scary.[135]

New York State Regent and testing advocate Meryl Tisch called opting out a "terrible mistake" because the tests allow parents to know how their children and their schools are doing. She likened opting out of tests to refusing to get an annual health check-up.[136] Amanda Ripley, author of *The Smartest Kids in the World,* tweeted sarcastically that if we are going to opt out of standardized tests, we should also opt out of vaccines and "lice checks."[137]

Other reformers have cast the debate as one about equity. These folks see annual standardized testing as part of an accountability system that forces teachers and schools to attend to the needs of the poor and minority children in (mostly) urban schools. As Chris Stewart, Director of Outreach and External Affairs for the reform-minded Education Post put it:

Renewed resistance to accountability is now a middle-class project to "reclaim" schools for a select slice of the American population who no longer want teachers and schools to be on the hook for results or equity.[138]

Similarly, Sonja Brookins Santelises, vice president of K-12 policy and practice for the Education Trust says:

We need a measure that allows us to get a snapshot that is consistent across communities and zip codes, that allows us to see where we are missing the mark for some groups of kids as opposed to others.[139]

Still other reformers see the threat to the education reform agenda that the opt out movement represents. Mike Petrilli, President of the pro-reform Thomas B. Fordham Institute, has said:

If this [opt out] thing goes national, the whole educa-

tion reform movement is in serious trouble.[140]

Perhaps recognizing this, Andy Smarick, writing in Fordham's *Common Core Watch* blog, takes a more conciliatory tone. He says:

> *I'm a strong supporter of assessments and accountability, and I wouldn't opt out. But I think it's unfair to discount the views of those who disagree, and it would be untoward to suggest they don't care about other kids or are insensitive to issues of race and income.*[141]

Opting-out of standardized testing is indeed a threat to the entire education reform agenda. The standardized test is the shaky foundation that this reform house is built upon. Corporate education reformers seem to be slowly waking up to this threat, and some are even showing a willingness to listen to concerned students, teachers and parents.

What are the consequences for my child of opting out of these standardized tests?

The consequences for the individual student of opting-out of Common Core aligned standardized tests are minimal. While the tests are high-stakes in the sense that they are used to grade the performance of a school or a school district or a teacher, they have not generally been used to grade children in any consequential way. Students are not required to pass the test to move to the next grade level, and high school students do not have to pass the test to graduate.

Testing advocates say that this new generation of tests will let parents know if their children are on the path to being "college and career ready", but no evidence has been provided to back up this claim. It is a claim built on the same flawed reasoning that went in to the Common Core. Teacher Peter Greene, writing in his blog, *Curmudgucation*, calls the reports that come out of Common Core aligned tests "vague and useless."[142]

These standardized tests can be used to provide some general information about what an individual child knows and can do, but usually higher quality information is available through a conference with the teacher and an examination of the work the child is doing in school. In fact, if a child is not developing as expected, a teacher may recommend some testing to get a sense of how to better help the child, but this type of targeted testing has proven to provide the kinds of specific information about individualized student learning needs that the Common Core aligned tests like PARCC and SBAC cannot.

Some states have tried to punish students who opt out by making the student as uncomfortable as possible during the testing situation. Some districts developed what is known as the "sit and stare" policy for students opting out. This means that the students would be required to sit in the testing room and stare at a blank screen. This policy was roundly condemned by parents and teacher organizations as abusive. In New Jersey, the legislature got involved and specifically forbade "sit and stare" policies. The legislature ordered schools to provide an educational program during testing for children who opt out.

About 14 states currently have legislation that requires third graders to pass a reading test to be promoted to fourth grade. Obviously, this makes that third grade reading test high-stakes indeed. This is an entirely inappropriate use of standardized testing that constitutes child abuse. Any decision about retention must be made through a collaborative discussion between parents, teachers, guidance counselors and administrators using class work, in-class assessments, and testing to make the decision. Standardized tests alone are simply not accurate enough to be the chief basis of these momentous decisions. Grade retention decisions should also be informed by the overwhelming research evidence that indicates that retention is generally not beneficial to children and often leads to dropping out of school.[143]

What are the consequences to my child's school and school district if my child opts out of the test?

Again, minimal. As the number of students opting out of the Common Core aligned standardized tests has grown, some testing advocates on the state level and the federal Department of Education have threatened that schools could lose federal funding if too many students opt out. According to Monty Neill of Fair Test, these threats are deliberately misleading. In fact, states that have laws allowing opting out (Utah, Wisconsin, Pennsylvania, Oregon, Washington, California and others on a growing list) have not faced any penalties whatsoever.[144]

There is no provision in any of the federal laws currently in place to deny funds to schools due to opting out. No states have ever lost any funding due to students opting out of testing, even though New York had a large number of opt outs in 2014 and 2015. The threats coming from state school superintendents and the U.S. Department of Education are intended to confuse parents considering opting out, because opting out is a very real threat to the corporate education reform movement's "test and punish" agenda for public education.

It is important to note that parents should check their local and state laws on testing, particularly for those tests, like the third grade literacy tests in some states, which are required for promotion or graduation. In these cases, where opting out has a direct impact on children, parents opposed to the testing may want to find other ways of objecting to the testing than opting out.

Should I opt out of standardized tests for my child?

Clearly, this is a very personal decision and one that each family must make on its own. Children, even very young children, need to be included in the decision making. Some kids like taking tests. Education historian and public education defender Diane Ravitch tells the story of her grandson, who looked forward to taking the tests because he was good at them and the tests gave him a chance to show off what he knew. Apparently, a year later he reconsidered because he told his grandmother that this year he was "opting-out."[145] If your child likes the type of challenge a test provides, you need to take that into your consideration.

It may be helpful to think about opting out as a way to exercise choice. Alan Singer of Hofstra University has suggested that people who can afford to send their children to exclusive private schools, like the Obamas who send their girls to the Washington DC Sidwell Friends School, are opting their children out because these schools do not use yearly standardized tests and do not use standardized tests to determine teacher or school quality.[146] So in one sense opting out is a choice that many make tacitly by choosing private or parochial school.

The most important thing that should drive the decision, however, is the long range view of how this test and punish reform design will impact your child's education. If you see the current focus on testing as a viable way to make sure that your child gets the best possible education, then you should have your child participate in the testing. On the other hand, if you believe a focus on testing is resulting in a narrowed curriculum in the school, with a lack of time for the more creative aspects of learning and with an unhealthy focus on test preparation, then you may want to protest this by opting out. Further, if you believe that children's standardized test scores are a poor way to evaluate teacher quality and school effectiveness, you may also wish to opt out.

If I choose to opt out of the test, how do I do it?

Several support groups have grown up around the opt out movement. The United Opt Out web site provides state-by-state guidelines for opting out, along with sample letters to be used for opting out, and the names and email addresses for people within your state that can advise you on opting out. The group also maintains a Facebook page called United Opt Out National and you can follow them on Twitter @UnitedOptOut.

The website Truth in American Education (truthinamerican-education.org) provides a concise overview of the issues related to opting out, state and local opt out regulations, sample opt out letters and a description of the process for making an opt out request. For more information about standardized testing in general, updates on the latest news on testing and the opt out movement you will also want to consult The National Center for Fair and Open Testing.

What resources can help me learn more about opting out?

If you are interested in taking an active role in the opt out movement, you will want to read this:

McDermott, M. and Robertson, P. (eds.). (2014). *An Activist Handbook for the Education Revolution: United Opt Out's Test of Courage*. Charlotte, NC: Information Age Publishing.

To hear the voice of teachers as it relates to standardized testing and opting out read these:

Hagopian, J. (2014). *More Than a Score: The New Uprising against High-Stakes Testing*. Chicago: Haymarket Books.

Vilson, J. (2014). *This Is Not A Test: A New Narrative on Race, Class, and Education*. Chicago: Haymarket Books.

These following websites provide information on testing as well as guides to opting out and sample letters to use if you decide to opt out:

The National Center for Fair and Open Testing. http://fairtest.org/get-involved/opting-out

Truth in American Education. http://truthinamericaneducation.com/

United Opt Out National. http://unitedoptout.com/

11

School Choice: Charter Schools and Vouchers

Isn't school choice a good thing?

What could be more American than choice? The country was founded on the principle of freedom of choice in speech, in religion, in the press, in assembly. Corporate education reformers tap into this most American of values by stating that parents, who after all pay for their child's education through taxes, should have choice in where they send their children to school. If a school is not performing well, and for the reformers this means the school is achieving low test scores, parents should have the right to choose a different school. As reformers are often heard to say, "zip code should not be destiny." In other words, where you go to school and the quality of the school you go to should not be determined by where you live.

For wealthy Americans, choice has always been available. Affluent parents have the option of sending their children to a private school of their choosing – a school that offers the type of curriculum and academic and social environment the parents find desirable. Less affluent middle-class families often exercise their choice by where they choose to live. I was once on a lengthy flight out of Newark, New Jersey's Liberty Airport, seated next to an Indian-American man who lived in northern New Jersey. We got into a conversation where I learned that he had two young children and I happened to mention the school district I worked in. The man said, "Oh yes, I know the district well, my wife and I are saving to move there because we have heard the schools are so good."

This story is repeated over and over throughout the country daily, and real estate agents are sure to include the quality of the schools in their sales pitch when the schools have a good reputation. Of course, a reputation for high quality schools means high housing costs and usually high property taxes. A large portion of the populace is effectively excluded from access to these "high-achieving" school districts by economic inequity.

Education reformers seek to emulate the choice enjoyed by the affluent and the upper middle class by offering the choice of the publicly funded, but privately run, charter school and the school voucher, which provides parents with money, again taken from public funds, to offset the cost of sending children to private institutions. If parents have such "choice", the reformers' story goes, public schools, charters and private schools will compete for public monies and all schools will improve their performance.

While all of this may sound good and may appeal to the American sense of freedom, civilized societies have long recognized that choice is not an absolute good. In America, we have the choice to smoke if we wish. I am old enough to remember entering the smoke-filled teachers' lounge in Bristol Jr.-Sr. High School in the 1970's. Smokers and non-smokers graded papers, planned lessons, held meetings and ate lunch in a haze of cigarette smoke that yellowed the fingers of the smokers and the formerly cream-colored walls of the cramped room.

Today, of course, we may still smoke if we wish, but we do not have the choice to smoke in the teachers' lounge or anywhere on school property for that matter. We have come to recognize that one person's choice to smoke may infringe on another person's choice to breathe clean air.

I am also old enough to remember when seat belts were first introduced into cars in the late fifties and how we were more likely to sit on them than strap them around our waists. Using the seat belt was a choice. While we can still make that choice, when we do so we are breaking the law and can be fined for failure to "buckle-up." The government came to realize that our choices needed to be limited for the public good. Seat belts saved lives and saved medical costs and so our choice was legislated away.

Like many of my generation, I was a vocal opponent of the Vietnam War. In those days there was much talk about choosing to withhold that part of our taxes that was being used to wage the war. Those who tried this were brought to court by the Internal Revenue Service. The courts, of course, ruled that because the government was charged by the Constitution to "provide for the common defense", the government had every right to collect my taxes for the military. I was free to choose to speak out against the war, assemble peacefully to protest the war, and write letters to the editor about the war, but I could not withhold my taxes. My choices were limited by law.

In our society we have come to recognize that choice is a good thing as long as it does not interfere with others' choices. What if an inner-city parent's choice is to send a child to a clean, safe, well-resourced, professionally staffed, neighborhood public school? By draining away the limited funds available for public education, charter schools and voucher schemes infringe on that parent's choice. It would be wise to spend our public tax monies on providing good local public schools. In public education, as with smoking and seatbelts and the military, the government must choose to limit our choice in order to provide for, as the Constitution says, "the common good." Public education is a common good that privatization in the form of charters and vouchers will destroy.

What is a charter school?

A charter school is an alternative public school where parents may choose to send their children and which operates without some of the regulations that are imposed on traditional public schools. A charter school must have its "charter", or plan of operation, approved by a local or state authorizing agency charged with reviewing the charter application. A charter authorization may be revoked after 3 to 5 years, if the authorizing agency finds that the school has not made adequate academic progress or if there are financial improprieties.

In theory, charter schools must accept all children who wish to attend, meet established academic progress goals, and be subject to audits of their use of public funds. According to the pro-charter group, The National Alliance for Public Charter Schools:

> *The core of the charter school model is the belief that public schools should be held accountable for student learning. In exchange for this accountability, school leaders should be given freedom to do whatever it takes to help students achieve and should share what works with the broader public school system so that all students benefit.*[147]

Charter schools typically receive their funds on a per-student basis. In other words, tax monies collected to support the public schools follow the child to the charter school. The amount charters get per student is generally between 70 and 90% of public school per student costs on the theory that charter schools do not incur some of the mandatory expenses imposed on traditional public schools

Charter schools are governed by an appointed board of directors, not an elected school board as is the case in most communities, or as in the case of many cities by a board appointed by the mayor or governor. Unlike these other boards, charter school boards are not required to conduct public business meetings, publish minutes or seek public input. Often times charter school board members are not members of the community they are serving.

The origins of the charter school movement began in the late 1980s, perhaps surprisingly, with Albert Shanker, the president of one of the large teacher unions, The American Federation of Teachers (AFT). Shanker envisioned a charter school as a place where:

> *... teachers would be given the opportunity to draw upon their expertise to create high-performing educational laboratories from which the public schools could learn.*[148]

He argued that charter schools could bring renewed vigor to the traditional goals of public education: social mobility and social integration. Critically, and inevitably, union leader Shanker also saw a central role for the teacher union in the design, development and implementation of charter schools.

The current charter school model is, however, very different from Shanker's ideal. Shanker's vision of "educational laboratories" closely tied to the public schools has evolved into a separate educational entity entirely. Supported by political conservatives and some social-justice minded Democrats on the left, charter schools have become the poster child for a "market driven" approach to school choice, and an opportunity to weaken teacher unions and teacher job protections. The innovative educational practices that Shanker hoped for have too often become joyless test preparation factories that rely on military style discipline practices and the employment of inexpensive and unqualified neophytes in teaching positions.

Why were charter schools created?

The charter school movement is a response to the perception coming out of *A Nation at Risk* and No Child Left Behind that America's public schools are not serving American children well. Of course, this perception is built on a large measure of reality. Even a cursory glimpse at the problems of urban schools like chronic underfunding, unsafe buildings in disrepair, discouraging drop-out rates, and limited opportunities for most children to go on to college reveals real concerns.

Less compelling as a reason for charter schools are the reports that America's schools are falling behind other nations, like Finland and China, and that this will lead to the country being unable to compete in a global economy. As Diane Ravitch has noted, this country has always scored in the middle of the pack on international tests like PISA since they were first given more than fifty years ago.[149] In all that time there has been no indication that America is falling behind other countries economically. What is true about national comparisons is that they point up the greatest challenge facing American education and a theme we return to over and over in this book – poverty and income inequity. When controlled for poverty, the United States finishes at or near the top on international test score comparisons.

Many people who start charter schools do so because they want to do good. They want to offer children and their parents an alternative to what they see as a failing system. It is also true that some charter operators, especially the large organizations running for-profit charters and online schools, are in the charter game for the money.[150] Other charter supporters, like the Walton Foundation, see the movement as part of a larger political effort to weaken unions, particularly the large and powerful teacher unions.[151] Whether a charter school operator has purely altruistic motives, base profit motives, or political motives, one thing that is true of all of them is that they are not being successful at improving America's educational prospects because they have not targeted the chief reason for low achievement – income inequity.

Are charter schools public schools?

The answer to this question depends on who you ask and when you ask the question. In many ways charter schools act like private schools. As Berliner and Glass have pointed out in their book *50 Myths and Lies that Threaten America's Schools*, unlike neighborhood public schools, charter schools can operate almost anywhere – on church property, out of a strip mall, out of a house, or even online. They often take on names that we would associate with private schools like "Success Academy" or "Foundations Preparatory School." Charter schools also do not report to a local school board as all traditional public schools must. They have "almost complete control over what they teach, how they teach, whom the hire and fire, and how they spend their money."[152]

Recent court decisions have also reinforced the idea that charter schools are private schools. When pressed to show financial records, some charter school operators have argued in court that they are private companies and are therefore not required to open their books. In a criminal case involving the fraudulent use of public funds brought against charter school operators in California, the

California Charter Schools Association argued that the defendants could not be prosecuted because they operated a private corporation.[153] In 2014, famed charter entrepreneur, Eva Moscowitz, filed suit against the state of New York saying that her Success Academy schools should not be subject to a state audit. She won the suit, which essentially said that Moscowitz's charter schools are a private entity separate from the state.[154]

Charter school operators seem to want to have it both ways. They are public schools when they line up for public funds to operate their schools. They are private schools whenever anyone wishes to look into how they are spending those funds. If a school is operating on public funds, it needs to be fiscally responsible to the taxpayers. Traditional public school budgets are rightfully subject to public review and comment, local public votes and yearly audits to ensure the schools are spending taxpayer's monies responsibly. Charter schools are public schools that should be required to demonstrate the same level of transparency. This is especially true as we have seen widespread reports of financial fraud perpetrated by charter school operators.[155] [156] [157]

What sorts of educational "innovation" do charter schools offer?

There are many different kinds of charter schools, including schools that focus on the arts, schools that focus on science and technology (so-called STEM schools), schools for children with disabilities, completely online schools where students study at home through a computer, and so-called "blended schools" that combine online learning with some classroom learning. While most charter schools are smaller than traditional public schools, and while some charter schools are locally developed and managed, many charter schools are part of a larger state, regional or national network of schools.

Except for some very important details, however, the vast majority of charter schools do not differ very much organizationally, instructionally or programmatically from a traditional public school. In the typical charter school children will have courses in English/language arts, mathematics, social studies, and science. Most charter schools will have physical education and music and art classes as well. Some charter schools develop their own curriculum, while others purchase curriculum from outside sources or use a curriculum developed by the parent company that runs the charter. Classes will be organized in grades PreK-12, with younger students in self-contained classrooms and students from 4th or 5th grade on up changing classes for different subjects. Students will typically be seated at desks or tables and they will be listening to a teacher or working in pairs or small groups. In other words, if you have been to school, you will recognize the structure of learning in a charter school.

The "innovations" that most charter schools provide are chiefly in the areas of establishing a culture focused on preparing to attend college, a behavior model based on military style discipline, and a curriculum focused on preparation for standardized tests. Here are the "five pillars" that form the foundation of the Knowledge is Power Program (KIPP) charter schools, one of the largest and most influential of the charter school models:[158]

- **High Achievement** – Students are expected to show high achievement in academics and conduct, and "no excuses" are accepted for failure to do so. A system of rewards and consequences is in place to ensure such high achievement.
- **Choice & Commitment** – Everyone (parents, teachers, students) must put in the time and effort required to achieve success.

- **More Time** – School days, school weeks and school years are all longer to help students achieve success.

- **Power to Lead** – Principals are given the power to make budgetary and staffing decisions quickly based on the school's needs.

- **Focus on Results** – This is a direct quote from the KIPP website: "*KIPP schools are relentlessly focused on high student performance on standardized tests and other objective measures.*"

I am sure that much of this sounds very good to many parents. Who could object to goals for high achievement? KIPP has been a highly influential charter model because its successes have been highly publicized. Laudatory reports on KIPP have been published in the Washington Post, New York Post, USA Today and broadcast on CNN, Fox News and NPR. A closer look inside KIPP schools paints a different picture, however.

Some of the KIPP innovations make sense. Some children need more time to learn. There is nothing inherently wrong with having high expectations, as long as those expectations are reasonable and achievable. Having the flexibility to provide that time and the staff committed to giving that time is educationally sound. It also makes sense to empower principals to make staffing and budgetary decisions without miles of red tape.

Other KIPP innovations are very problematic. The "no excuses" philosophy, combined with achievement defined by standardized test scores, means that instruction will be narrowed to focus on improving test scores. When standardized test scores drive instruction and curriculum, the instruction can be overly teacher driven and the curriculum tends to be limited to those areas that are tested. This has, in fact, been the case. The Success Academies schools in

New York City, which use a similar "no-excuses" model as KIPP Schools, have shown some extraordinary success (i.e. they have been successful in raising children's test scores). They have also shown an educational environment built on harsh discipline, high teacher turnover and large numbers of students dropping out or being counseled out.[159]

Dr. Anne Evans de Bernard, a school principal in Connecticut, has characterized the "no excuses" educational approach as "colonialism."[160] In other words, a program developed by the largely white dominant culture and inflicted on the largely brown and black minority culture. In "no-excuses" schools minor infractions are often punished harshly. Children's desks are moved away from others and miscreants must eat at a separate table in the lunch room. As I wrote in a blog post on the issue, I have personally witnessed this approach in a "no-excuses" charter school.

> *In a "no excuses" school I visited, all the students wore blue shirts and khaki pants. I noticed that while this was nearly universal, a few children had on yellow t-shirts over their blue shirts. When I inquired about this, I was told that these children were being punished for talking in class or the hallway or for disrupting class in some way. They were "on the bench" and the yellow shirts identified them as such. Yellow shirts! Wear your shame for all to see. I guess Walmart was out of dunce caps.*[161]

The shaming of students does not stop with discipline policies. In many charter schools, including those I have visited, student test scores are publicly displayed on "data walls" that show everyone coming in or going from the school who has scored well and who has not scored well.[162] Any effective school must have discipline policies and an orderly environment for learning, but establishing such an environment through draconian punishments and public shaming is not acceptable. I doubt highly that a suburban public school could ever get away with this.

Not all charter schools follow the KIPP model and certainly not all follow the "no excuses" approach, but KIPP schools have received much positive publicity and have been held up as a model to emulate,[163] so it is important to understand what "no excuses" means. We must also ask if this "innovation" is one that is desirable for public schools, which charter schools purport to be.

Another charter school innovation involves the use of technology. The past several years have seen the growth of K-12 online schools and so-called blended schools, which combine online learning with some classroom instruction. Traditional public schools have been slow to adopt the educational possibilities of the digital world, so many reformers and parents have welcomed the "innovations" promised by online and blended school models. Computer-based models of education have proved to be attractive to families who home school children and to families whose children have not had good experiences in traditional schooling.

Some education reformers are attracted to online learning models because they are cheaper. Online schools require much less investment in brick and mortar buildings than traditional schools. The costs of staffing online charter schools is also greatly lowered because teachers can "handle" many more students than a classroom teacher during any instructional period. Online charters also have the potential to provide huge markets for the manufacturers of online course software and computer hardware.

The conservative think-tank, The Heritage Foundation, is particularly bullish on the idea of online learning. In a 2010 policy paper they declared in part

> *[O]nline learning is revolutionizing American education. It has the potential to dramatically expand the educational opportunities of American students, largely overcoming the geographic and demographic restrictions. Virtual learning also has the potential to improve the quality of instruction, while increasing productivity and lowering costs, ultimately reducing the burden on taxpayers.*[164]

Other groups do not share The Heritage Foundation's enthusiasm. The National Education Policy Center (NEPC) looked closely at the largest online school provider in the country, K12, Inc. This company has online schools in many states and consistently shows lower learning gains than traditional schools, as measured by standardized tests in both math and reading. The lower scores in math are particularly interesting because math scores are more susceptible to instruction than reading scores, which tend to be more related to parenting and home environment. NEPC explains the reasons for the low achievement scores as follows:

> *Based on our findings, K12 devotes considerably fewer resources to instructional salaries and benefits for employees. This reduced spending on salaries is linked to the fact that K12 has more than three times the number of students per teacher compared with overall public school student-teacher ratios. The higher student-teacher ratio and the reduced spending on teacher salaries, as well as on salaries for all other categories of staff typically found in schools, help explain the poor performance of K12's schools.*[165]

Because charter schools have fewer restrictions than traditional public schools they have also been able to "innovate" in the areas of staffing and teacher salaries. While in some states teachers in charter schools must be certified teachers, and typically this means that the person has at least a bachelor's degree (normally in education), has studied both content and teaching practice, and has done some practice teaching under the guidance of an experienced mentor, many states have loosened the rules for certification over the past 20 years. A few states, like North Carolina and Kansas, have made it possible to teach in high poverty districts without any teaching certification at all. This loosening of standards has allowed many charter schools to hire uncertified or marginally certified teachers.

Many charters have relied on staffing through Teach for America (TFA), a program originally designed to recruit recent college graduates to help staff schools that had teacher shortages, but that is now used largely as an alternative staffing provider for charter schools in urban areas. The educational impact of TFA was dealt with in detail in Chapter 7, but for now we can define TFA as a program that recruits prospective teachers from college campuses, where they have been pursuing degrees in fields other than education, provides the recruits with 5 weeks of teacher training in the summer, and then offers these recruits to charter schools to fill teaching vacancies.

Charter school teacher salary innovation has taken the form of merit pay, which pays those teachers identified as more effective more money through bonuses or increased salaries, seeking to emulate private business practices of rewarding high performers and punishing low performers. In contrast, in traditional public schools teacher pay increases are tied to years of experience and higher levels of education. Like all aspects of the reform agenda, standardized tests play a large role in determining which teachers are effective and which are not.

Proponents of merit pay say that the system will motivate

teachers to do their best work because that work will be financially rewarded. Former Washington, DC schools chancellor and noted education reformer, Michelle Rhee has said that merit pay will help attract better teacher candidates to inner cities saying, "we have to make [teaching] a profession that high achievers want to go into."[166] Critics of merit pay, who include the teacher unions, worry that the system will create unhealthy competition in a profession that thrives on cooperation, and that it is impossible to parse out a teacher's impact on a child's learning when so many outside factors are involved.

Charter schools have provided innovations through carrot and stick approaches to student motivation and discipline, through a heavy focus on standardized test scores and data, through online schools, through the increased use of teachers with limited experience and training, and in basing pay on "merit" measured by student performance on standardized tests. After 20 years, few of these "innovations" have taken hold in the traditional public schools. While this may be because traditional schools are resistant to change, it is more likely due to many of these innovations being unacceptable to those who send their children to traditional public schools.

Do charter schools do a better job educating children than traditional public schools?

According to Jim Hull, Senior Policy Analyst for the Center for Public Education, "overall charter schools do no better or worse than traditional public schools."[167] About 17% of charter schools performed significantly better than their neighborhood traditional schools, 37% of charters performed significantly worse, and the remaining 46% performed about the same. Research also shows that students in charter high schools scored higher on college entrance exams and were more likely to graduate. Results vary a great deal from state to state.

Newspapers, television, and even films are, of course, full of reports of the heroic successes of some charter schools. There is no question that some charters have been successful in raising test scores for some children. In a Forbes Magazine article, Adam Ozemick, citing a study done by Stanford's Center for Research on Education Outcomes (CREDO), argues that charter schools have been shown to be more effective for students in poverty than traditional schools. Ozemick further argues that charter schools are improving over time.[168] The National Education Policy Center also looked at the CREDO report and concluded that the findings of greater effectiveness of charter schools for children in poverty were overstated and not a worthy basis for policy decisions.[169]

Of course, everyone weighing in on the charter school success question has an agenda. If you are pro-charter you tend to view the research in the most positive light. If you are anti-charter your tendency is to view the research in the most negative light. The truth generally lies somewhere in-between. Charter schools have likely been effective for some students, but overall their performance has been about the same as traditional public schools. It is also important to remember that performance in these research studies is based almost exclusively on standardized test scores in math and language arts – a very narrow measure of school performance.

What is the impact of charter schools on traditional public schools?

The failure of charter schools to produce significant improvements in student performance takes on more importance when the impact of charters on traditional schools is taken into account.

David Hornbeck, former superintendent of schools in Philadelphia and in the state of Maryland, was an early supporter of charter schools. In the 1990s he approved the opening of 30 charter schools in Philadelphia. Since then he has changed his mind about charters. He gave his reasons in an opinion piece in The Baltimore Sun. Besides not showing significant educational improvement, he said:

- Charter schools are draining money from public schools.
- Charter schools do not serve the students with the greatest needs.
- Strong charter laws undermine teacher unions and teacher job protections guaranteeing that we will not be attracting the best and brightest to teaching positions.[170]

When children leave the traditional public school to attend a charter, the money allocated to educate those children goes to the charter school. In theory this would make sense, because the charter school would then use the money to educate the child and the public school would not have the cost of educating that child. In reality, however, losing a child or 20 children or 100 children to a charter does not proportionately reduce the costs of running a school. Even if 100 students leave, the school must still be cleaned, heated, and maintained. Also, support staff must be provided, and costly state and federal mandates must be met. Many schools, especially the urban schools most impacted by charters, were already struggling mightily with underfunding even before the advent of charter schools, which have exacerbated their underfunding. In fact Moody's Investment Service issued this warning to investors considering buying city bonds:

> *This dramatic rise in charter school enrollments over the past decade is likely to create negative credit pressure on school districts in economically weak urban*

areas.[171]

The economic impact is compounded by the failure of charter schools to accept children with special learning needs. In theory, and by law, charter schools are required to accept any and all comers to their schools, just as any public school would be expected to do. In practice, however, this has not proved to be the case. University of Colorado Professor Kevin Welner has discovered multiple ways that charters shape their student populations. Here are some highlights:[172]

- Marketing that emphasizes "college prep" and "rigorous curriculum" will attract higher achieving students.
- Marketing brochures that are only in English will discourage parents of English Language Learners from signing up.
- Providing short time windows for applications.
- Requiring parent volunteer activities or parent visitations.
- Enforcing harsh discipline policies that eliminate students through repeated suspensions.
- Failing to provide needed special education services.
- "Counseling out" students who are not performing well.
- Placing grade point or course restrictions on eligible applicants.
- Steering students with disabilities away because the public school is better able to provide for their needs.
- Threatening the parents and child with being retained in the current grade.

The result of these student skimming practices is to leave the public school with a higher concentration of students who have special needs and the costs needed to provide for these children at the same time that the coffers are being drained by the charter schools.

The vast majority of charter schools are non-union and do not provide for teacher tenure or seniority protections. This is supposed to allow the school leaders the flexibility to fire and hire at will in order to get the best teachers in place. As Hornbeck points out, however, unionism is not the problem. There are very strong unions in some of our highest performing states, and many, many of the lowest performing states have no teacher unions. Schools that limit teacher job protections will have difficulty attracting the best and brightest teachers to work in the schools, and will also have difficulty holding onto those teachers.[173] In fact, teacher attrition in charter schools is very high. While numerous studies have found different rates of teachers leaving charter schools, the consensus is that figuring in all factors, teachers voluntarily leave charter schools at a rate about 33% higher than teachers in traditional public schools.[174] High levels of attrition, of course, mean that a school has difficulty maintaining continuity of programs and consistency in instruction.

The non-union and often anti-union approach taken by charter schools has indirectly but inevitably led to reduced teacher protections in traditional public schools. Assaults on such job protections as tenure and seniority have become commonplace.[175] Again, as Hornbeck notes, these policies will make it harder for traditional public schools to attract the best teachers.[176]

In many ways charter schools and charter school legislation are making it harder for traditional public schools to do their job. This is not to say that traditional public schools in all areas were doing their job well, but only that charter schools, as currently formulated, are simply the wrong answer to a very complex problem.

Should I send my child to a charter school?

If I were answering this question from a purely big picture perspective, considering the overall impact of charter schools on the ability of traditional public schools to deliver a high quality education, the answer to this question would be a quick and assured, "No." However, if I am answering this question from a parent's perspective, the answer is much more complex. In the long run, I believe society would be better off to invest its resources intelligently in traditional public schools. Individual children do not have a long run, however, so what is a parent to do?

The education reform minded Thomas B. Fordham Institute conducted a survey to determine what parents want from a school.[177] They reported that nearly all parents wanted a school with a strong basic curriculum in language arts and mathematics. They also wanted schools that provided strong science and technology programs, and focused on strong verbal and written communication skills, critical thinking, and good study habits. Beyond this general agreement the Fordham report broke down parents into "Pragmatists" who wanted strong vocational training, "Jeffersonians" who wanted an emphasis on good citizenship, "Test-score Hawks" who focused on high test scores, "Expressionists" who wanted a strong arts education focus, "Multi-culturists" who wanted children to learn to get along with people from different backgrounds, and "Strivers" who wanted a school that provided a path to a "top-tier" college.

I am sure each of these labels capture what many people want from a school, but I think it ignores some of the most basic desires that parents want for their children. I think parents want, most of all, for their children to attend a safe, clean, welcoming school where their children feel comfortable and secure. Secondly, I believe that parents want a school that is nurturing; one that recognizes the uniqueness of each child, and one that provides a warm, friendly, and intellectually stimulating place to grow. Parents also want a school where the resources for learning are available through adequate staffing, including teachers, counselors, nurses and librarians, adequate learning resources like books, libraries and technology, and adequate extra-curricular programs in the arts and in sports. Further, parents want a school where they are kept in the loop, where communication between school and parent and teacher and parent is regular and informative, and helps answer the questions, "How is my kid doing?" and "Is my kid happy?" Finally, parents want the school to be a local neighborhood school, but if that kind of school is not available locally, they will look elsewhere.

I would argue that every local neighborhood school can and should be able to provide this kind of education for every child. I would also argue that parents should fight to make sure that their neighborhood school gets the resources to make it the kind of school all families want to send their child to. But when that school is not provided locally, it is reasonable to expect a parent to investigate charter schools. What should a parent look for in a charter school? Here are a few questions to ask before choosing a charter school:

- What is the charter's mission statement? Does this mission statement align with what I want for my child?
- What will the day-to-day life of my child be like in this charter school?
- Is the school clean and safe?
- Does the school provide a nurturing environment?
- Does the school employ certified teachers? What is the average level of experience of the teachers? What is the rate of teacher turnover?

- Is the school leadership readily available and responsive to parents' needs and concerns?
- Is the school's website regularly updated and is the school calendar current?
- Does all evidence suggest the school is well-organized and effectively managed?
- Does the data available provide good information on how the school is doing academically in general and in my child's particular grade specifically?
- Does the school offer a broad variety of programs that will interest my child?
- What is the school's discipline policy? Does this match with my own ideas of appropriate discipline?
- Does the school have a good track record built up over the years? What do other parents say about their experience with the school?
- What is the average class size?
- How does the school support students who have academic, social or emotional challenges?
- Does the school offer a physical education program?
- Does the school offer a rich and varied arts program?
- How is technology used to support instruction?

I recognize that parents may deem it necessary to choose a charter school as the best choice for their child who cannot wait for overall school improvement in the local traditional public school. I also hope that parents, having an understanding of how the entire charter movement is ultimately destructive to the concept of a free and first rate system of public education, will work on the long range goals of ensuring that local, neighborhood public schools get the resources they need to be successful no matter what neighborhood they are in.

What is a school voucher?

School vouchers, which may also be known as opportunity scholarships or education tax credits, are state-funded checks that can be used to send children to private schools, charter schools, parochial schools, or public schools other than the one to which the children would ordinarily be assigned. The money to support vouchers comes, of course, from the same pot of money that is used to support public schools. School vouchers are the brain child of the economist Milton Friedman, who in the 1950s posited that a voucher system would create competition which would improve schools and create efficiency.[178]

Vouchers have a rather tawdry early history because they were used in many southern states in the wake of the Supreme Court's *Brown v. Board of Education* decision of 1954, which ruled that segregated schools were unconstitutional. Some southern states attempted to get around the ruling by closing the public schools and providing families with vouchers so they could "choose" private segregated schools.[179]

In the 21st century, the school voucher has become a tool of those education reformers who see choice as the best way to improve public schools. In 2014, the Center for Education Reform, a pro-voucher group, looked at the voucher laws in all the states and rated the states by the strength of such laws. States with the strongest voucher laws were Indiana, Ohio, Wisconsin, North Carolina and

Louisiana.[180] Each of these states has a conservative Republican governor and a legislature dominated by Republicans. Only the District of Columbia cracked the top 10 of voucher states without a full Republican majority in the state house. Since that study was published, Nevada has passed perhaps the most comprehensive voucher program in the country, calling them Education Savings Accounts. Nevada, you guessed it, has a Republican governor, and Republicans are in the majority in the state legislature. So clearly, vouchers are popular with especially those Republicans who buy into Friedman's concept of improving schooling on the cheap through competition.

Critics of vouchers include a coalition of disparate groups including teacher unions, the American Civil Liberties Union, the Education Law Center and religious organizations like the Baptist Joint Committee for Religious Liberty. A compilation of the concerns about school vouchers includes the following: [181]

- Vouchers will never include enough money for a child from a poor or even lower middle income to go to expensive private schools.
- Vouchers take money directly from public school funding. Public schools will, therefore, fall further behind in providing the kinds of programs and resources that their students need.
- Vouchers amount to a give-away to wealthy and upper middle class families who will use them to subsidize the private school tuition they would choose to pay for anyway.
- Vouchers force Americans to pay taxes to support religion. Vouchers could well be used to underwrite student attendance at religious schools – a violation of the separation of church and state.

- Under voucher systems, private schools can accept vouchers, but can still practice exclusionary practices, religious and racial discrimination, only admitting those they choose.
- Private schools are not subject to the same accountability for programs or for finances as are public schools.
- Vouchers do not improve opportunities for low income children. In Cleveland for example, parents who were granted vouchers, but failed to use them, reported that the additional costs, like the balance of the tuition, transportation, supplies, and uniforms kept them from using their vouchers.
- Vouchers distract from the real issue of reform. Most public schools do a very good job, and those that don't need help, not abandonment.

In August of 2014, North Carolina's voucher law was tested in the state courts. Judge Robert Hobgood struck down the law declaring:

> *Private schools receiving Opportunity Scholarships are not subject to any requirements or standards regarding the curriculum that they teach, are given no requirement for student achievement, are not obligated to demonstrate any growth in student performance, and are not even obligated to provide a minimum amount of instructional time.*[182]

He further observed that the voucher law did not require that the recipient schools "provide their students with instruction in any subject," or that teachers or principals "be trained, certified, or qualified," or that the schools themselves be "certified by any public or private agency." He concluded that the state legislature "fails the children of North Carolina when they (are) sent with public taxpayer money to private schools that have no legal obligation to teach them anything." Such a scheme "serves only private interests."[183]

Do vouchers work in improving the quality of education?

As you might expect, the answer to this question depends on who you ask, but some tentative conclusions can be reached. The Milwaukee School Choice Program has the longest history of any school voucher program. The Milwaukee Journal Sentinel reported the following in March 2011:

> *A day after the release of state test scores showed voucher-school students in Milwaukee achieving lower levels of reading and math proficiency than students in Milwaukee Public Schools, new data from researchers studying the voucher program's results over multiple years shows those students are doing about the same as MPS students, not worse.*[184]

And then in April 2014 the Journal Sentinel reported:

> *On average, students in Milwaukee's private-school voucher program still performed lower than students in the city's traditional public school system.*[185]

Another study, out of the University of Arkansas Department of Educational Reform, which is heavily funded by the Walton Foundation and decidedly pro-school choice, looked at three years of data and found that vouchers students were not doing worse, but were certainly not doing any better.[186] Despite this evidence, Governor Scott Walker of Wisconsin decided to ask the legislature to expand the voucher program in the next budget.[187] One needs to wonder if vouchers are sound educational policy or purely political policy.

The DC Opportunity Scholarship Program, which was signed into law by President George W. Bush in 2005, was monitored yearly by the Department of Education. The DOE reported that the program did not have much of an impact. According to the Huffington Post, the DOE study showed that:

> *... students applying to the program from schools in need of improvement (SINI), which were labeled as highest priority by Congress, had no achievement impacts.*[188]

Even President Obama, generally a fan of the education reform agenda, opposes vouchers, saying in a statement of administration policy addressed to House Majority Leader, John Boehner:

> *... [p]rivate school vouchers are not an effective way to improve student achievement.*[189]

Do school vouchers work to improve educational outcomes and streamline spending? The growing consensus is a resounding, "No!" The Nevada law will be particularly devastating to the public schools of that state which are already grossly underfunded. Nevada ranks 40th out of 50 states in terms of public school funding. Jennifer Berkshire, author of the popular blog *Edushyster*, has said that the Nevada voucher law will:

> *... not only leave problems like overcrowding and deterioration unaddressed, but will actually leave the majority of kids in Nevada's schools worse off.*[190]

Should I consider homeschooling my child?

Nationwide over 2 million children are homeschooled, a

number that has grown exponentially in the last 20 years. The number one reason children are homeschooled is parental religious and values preferences, but other parents choose homeschooling because they are not satisfied with the public schools available to them or because they feel their child's needs are not being met in the public schools.[191]

Homeschooling is a choice parents may make in all 50 states in the United States. States vary in the amount of oversight they require of homeschooling parents. Ten states require no notice and provide no reporting of homeschoolers, while five other states have extensive regulations for homeschooling. Most states fall somewhere in the middle, requiring some notification, but providing little oversight. To find out what the laws are in your state you can look at the Home Schooling Legal Defense Association (HSLDA) website.[192]

The key question, of course, is not whether you can legally homeschool, but whether you should. In order to answer this question, you must first determine what kind of commitment you are willing to make as a parent. There is little question that homeschooling can be successful, but the key variable in successful homeschooling is parental involvement in the process. About 95% of homeschooled children are taught by a stay at home parent. Homeschooling is a full time job, so a family must determine if it is possible to forego a second income in order to homeschool.

Parents must also decide if they have the academic wherewithal to provide the education their children deserve. While research on homeschooling is sparse, some studies have indicated that overall, homeschoolers do better than regular school students in reading, but less well in math.[193] While it is not clear why this might be true, parents need to ask themselves how able they are to provide instruction in the broad spectrum of subjects that a school provides. This concern may deepen once students advance past the elementary grades and need instruction in complex concepts in literacy, social studies, mathematics, and science.

Some educators and even some homeschooling advocates worry about the isolation of homeschooling and the impact of this isolation on a child's ability to interact with peers. Studies have found that homeschooled children can be very well socialized, but again the socialization depends on the parents' willingness to ensure that this socialization happens.[194] Homeschooled children need to be involved in outside the home activities like field trips with other children, group sports, dance classes, drama clubs, and music classes in order to develop healthy relationships with peers. Even for parents who ensure these experiences for their children, the peer group the child encounters is often not as diverse as the peer groups in the local school, so concerns about the breadth of the socialization remain.

Homeschooling success stories and homeschooling horror stories can readily be found all over the internet. Homeschooling advocate groups, of course, focus on the positive, while opponents highlight the negative. What can be said with certainty is that any family making the decision to homeschool must be fully committed to the needs of their children in this process and willing to put those needs before all else. They must also be willing to develop a structured and varied program of learning that provides the curriculum, the instruction and the time necessary to meet their children's needs.

What resources can help me learn more about school choice?

For a book length analysis of how school choice impacts

public schools read this:

Ravitch, D. (2010). *The death and life of the great American school system*. NY: Basic Books.

For a book length comparison of private school and public school performance try this:

Lubienski, C. and Lubienski, S.T. (2013). *The public school advantage; Why public schools outperform private schools*. Chicago: University of Chicago Press.

For a look at what the research says about the impact of school choice please see:

Berliner. D. and Glass, G. (2014). *50 myths and lies that threaten America's schools*. NY: Teachers College Press.

For an excellent article length analysis of the charter school impact on public education see:

Karp, S. (2013). Charter schools and the future of public education. *Rethinking Schools*. Volume 28 No. 1. http://www.rethinkingschools.org/archive/28_01/28_01_karp.shtml

For a slightly dated, but still useful look at the research on school choice please read this research brief:

Gill, B., Timpane, P. M., Ross, K.E. and Brewer, D. J. (2007). *Rhetoric Versus Reality: What We Know and What We Need to Know about Vouchers and Charter Schools*. Santa Monica, CA: Rand Education. http://www.rand.org/pubs/monograph_reports/MR1118-1.html

References

1. Ravitch, D. (2010). *The Death and Life of the Great American School System: How Testing and Choice Are Undermining Education.* NY: Basic Books. https://www.goodreads.com/work/quotes/7189253-the-death-and-life-of-the-great-american-school-system

2. Katz, M. (2001). *The Irony of Early School Reform: Education Innovation in Mid-Nineteenth Century Massachusetts.* 2nd Edition. NY: Teachers College Press.

3. U. S. Department of Education. (1983) *A Nation at Risk.* Retrieved from https://www2.ed.gov/pubs/NatAtRisk/risk.html

4. Carson, C.C., Huelskamp, C.M., & Woodall, T.D. Perspectives on Education in America: An Annotated Briefing. *Journal of Educational Research.* 86 (May/June 1993), 260-310.

5. Stedman, L. C. (1994). The Sandia Report and U. S. Achievement: An Assessment. *Journal of Educational Research.* 87(3). Retrieved from http://www.jstor.org/stable/27541911?seq=1#page_scan_tab_contents

6. Ansary, T. (March 9, 2007). Education at Risk: Fallout from a Flawed Report. *Edutopia.* Retrieved from http://www.edutopia.org/landmark-education-report-nation-risk

7. The Bill and Melinda Gates Foundation. (2009). *Annual Letter.* Retrieved from https://docs.gatesfoundation.org/Documents/2009-bill-gates-annual-letter.pdf

8. Schneider, M.K. (2014). *A Chronicle of Echoes.* Charlotte, NC: Information Age Publishing.

9. The Walton Family Foundation. (n.d.). *Creating Opportunity So Individuals and Communities Can Live Better in Today's World.* Retrieved from http://dbd7853403f6a0e4167e-9fe3b5899f298e1c7d591332d27bb114.r52.cf1.rackcdn.com/documents/46315af7-4637-4c25-b288-0c141ee94cbb.pdf

10. Schneider, M.K. (2014). op.cit.

11. Allen, S. (August 27, 2015). Is Teach for America Flunking Out. *The Daily Beast.* Retrieved from http://www.thedailybeast.com/articles/2015/08/27/is-teach-for-america-flunking-out.html

12. Students First. (2013). *Policy Report Card.* Retrieved from http://edref.3cdn.net/9e8505b2c4ad5ec0e8_u6m6ikky8.pdf

13. Strauss, V. (Nov. 15, 2011). Ravitch: Billionaires (and millionaires) for education reform. *The Washington Post.* Retrieved from https://www.washingtonpost.com/blogs/answer-sheet/post/ravitch-billionaires-and-millionaires-for-education-reform/2011/11/15/gIQAlDAHPN_blog.html

14. Russakoff, D. (2015). *The Prize: Who's in Charge of America's Schools?* NY: Houghton Mifflin Harcourt.

15. The Center for Research on Evaluation, Standards & Student Testing. (1994). A Guide to Parents and Communities Seeking Excellence in Education. *UCLA Graduate School of Education.* Retrieved from https://www.cse.ucla.edu/products/parents/cresst_GoodSchool.pdf

16. Schools of Opportunity. (n.d.). Retrieved from http://opportunitygap.org/selection-criteria.html

17. Popham, W. J. (n.d*.). Uses and Misuses of Standardized Achievement Tests.* Retrieved from http://www.ioxassessment.com/download/UsesandMisusesofStandardized.pdf

18. Gewertz, C. (February 18, 2014). "Platooning" on the Rise in Early Grades. *Education Week.* Retrieved from http://www.edweek.org/ew/articles/2014/02/19/21department.h33.html

19. Strauss, V. (March 14, 2014). How 'platooning' and data walls are changing elementary school. *The Washington Post.* Retrieved from https://www.washingtonpost.com/blogs/answer-sheet/wp/2014/03/14/how-platooning-and-data-walls-are-changing-elementary-school/

20. Coggins, C. and Hassel, B. (October 26, 2012). Expanding the Impact of Excellent Teachers. *Education Next.* Retrieved from http://educationnext.org/expanding-the-impact-of-excellent-teachers/

21. Center for Public Education (n.d*.). Class size and student achievement: Research Review.* Retrieved from http://www.centerforpubliceducation.org/Main-Menu/Organizing-a-school/Class-size-and-student-achievement-At-a-glance/Class-size-and-student-achievement-Research-review.html#sthash.EEnIMv1M.dpuf

22. Schanzenbach, D.W. (2014). Does Class Size Matter? Boulder, CO: *National Education Policy Center.* Retrieved from http://nepc.colorado.edu/publication/does-class-size-matter

23. National Association of Elementary School Principals. (2013). What the Research Says About the Importance of Principal Leadership. *Leadership Matters.* Retrieved from http://www.naesp.org/sites/default/files/LeadershipMatters.pdf

24. McIver, M.C., Kearns, J., Lyons, C., & Sussman, M. (2009). *Leadership: A McREL report prepared for Stupski Foundation's Learning System.* Denver, CO: Mid-continent Research for Education and Learning. Retrieved from http://files.eric.ed.gov/fulltext/ED544625.pdf

25. National Association of Elementary Principals, op. cit.

26. RTI Action Network. (n.d.). *What is RTI?* Retrieved from http://www.rtinetwork.org/learn/what/whatisrti

27. National Association of School Nurses. (n.d.). Healthy Children Learn Better! School Nurses Make a Difference. *Nursing World.* Retrieved from http://nursingworld.org/DocumentVault/GOVA/Ruler-FAQ.pdf

28. American School Counselor Association. (n.d.). *The Role of the Professional School Counselor.* Retrieved from http://www.schoolcounselor.org/asca/media/asca/home/rolestatement.pdf

29. MacMeekin, M. (April 12, 2013). 27 Things your Teacher/Librarian Does. *An Ethical Island* blog. Retrieved from https://anethicalisland.wordpress.com/2013/04/12/27-things-your-teacher-librarian-does/

30. Maxwell, K., & R.M. Clifford. (2004). Research in review: School readiness assessment. *Young Children* 59 (1): 42. Retrieved from https://www.naeyc.org/files/naeyc/file/positions/Readiness.pdf

31. Iowa University Extension. (September 29, 2009). First Grade: Ready or Not? *Education.com.* Retrieved from http://www.education.com/reference/article/first-grade-ready-not/

32. National Association for the Education of Young Children, (n.d.). *Developmentally Appropriate Practice.* Retrieved from http://www.naeyc.org/DAP

33. Bodrova, E. & Leong, D. J. (2007). *Tools of the mind: The Vygotskian approach to early childhood education (2nd Ed.).* Columbus, OH: Merrill/Prentice Hall. P. 142.

34. National Association for the Education of Young Children, op. cit.

35. National Association for the Education of Young Children. (2009). *Developmentally Appropriate Practice in Early Childhood Programs Serving Children from Birth through Age 8: Position Statement.* Retrieved from https://www.naeyc.org/files/naeyc/file/positions/position%20statement%20Web.pdf

36. California Department of Education. (n.d.). *Developmentally Responsive*

Middle School Practices. Retrieved from http://pubs.cde.ca.gov/tcsii/ch4/devresponmgprctces.aspx

37. Gest, S.D., Freeman, N.R., Domitrovich, C.E. & Welsh, J.A. (2004). Shared book reading and children's language comprehension skills: the moderating role of parental discipline practices. *Early Childhood Research Quarterly.* 19, 319-336. Retrieved from http://www.sciencedirect.com/science/article/pii/S0885200604000432

38. Rowe, K. (1991). The influence of reading activity at home on students' attitudes towards reading, classroom attentiveness and reading achievement: An application of structural equation modelling. *British Journal of Educational Psychology*. 61, 19-35. Retrieved from https://www.researchgate.net/publication/229674963

39. Baker, L. & Scher, D. (2002). Beginning readers' motivation for reading in relation to parental beliefs and home reading experiences. *Reading Psychology*. 23, 239-269. Retrieved from https://www.researchgate.net/publication/240238647

40. Mullis, R.L., Mullis, A.K., Cornille, T.A., Ritchson, A.D. & Sullender, M.S. (2004). *Early literacy outcomes and parent involvement*. Tallahassee, FL: Florida State University. Retrieved from http://www.chs.fsu.edu/content/download/68056/753830/file/hubs_study_final_report_5_28_04.pdf

41. Taylor, D. (1998). *Family Literacy: Young Children Learning to Read and Write*. Portsmouth, NH: Heinemann Drama.

42. Heath, S. B. (1982). What no bedtime story means: Narrative skills at home and school. *Language in Society.* II, 49-76. Retrieved from http://people.ucsc.edu/~gwells/Files/Courses_Folder/documents/Heath.BedtimeStories.pdf

43. Mershon, C. (2015). Captioned Television: Developing Readers at School and at Home. *Russ on Reading* blog. Retrieved from http://russonreading.blogspot.com/2015/06/captioned-television-developing-readers.html

44. University of Michigan. (2015). *Debunking the Myths of Dyslexia*. Retrieved from http://dyslexiahelp.umich.edu/dyslexics/learn-about-dyslexia/what-is-dyslexia/debunking-common-myths-about-dyslexia

45. University of Michigan. (2015). *Principles of Effective Dyslexia Intervention.* Retrieved from http://dyslexiahelp.umich.edu/parents/learn-about-dyslexia/dyslexia-treatment/principles-effective-dyslexia-treatment

46. Strauss, S.L. Goodman, K.S. and Paulsen, E. J. (2009). Brain research and reading: How emerging concepts in neuroscience support a meaning construction view of the reading process. *Educational Research and Review.* Vol. 4 (2), pp. 021-033. Retrieved from http://ericpaulson.wp.txstate.edu/files/2014/05/strauss_goodman_paulson_2009.pdf

47. Krech, B. (2015). Personal communication.

48. Ibid.

49. Ibid

50. Ibid.

51. Parenting Horizons. (n.d.) *When Children Aren't Appropriately Challenged.* Retrieved from http://www.parentinghorizons.com/node/169

52. Elias, M., et al. (1997). *Promoting Social and Emotional Learning.* Alexandria, VA: ASCD. Retrieved from http://www.ascd.org/publications/books/197157/chapters/The-Need-for-Social-and-Emotional-Learning.aspx

53. Goleman, D. (2005). *Emotional Intelligence: Why It Can Matter More Than IQ.* New York: Bantam Books.

54. Carnegie Council on Adolescent Development. (1989). *Turning points: Preparing American youth for the 21st century: The report of the task force on the education of young adolescents.* Washington, D.C.: Carnegie Council on Adolescent Development.

55. Parker, J. D. and Summerfeldt, L. J. (March 25, 2014). Emotional Intelligence and Academic Success: Examining the Transition from High School to University. *Research Gate.* Retrieved from http://www.researchgate.net/publication/247166939_Emotional_Intelligence_and_Academic_Success_Examining_the_Transition_from_High_School_to_University

56. Responsive Classroom. (2015). *What is Morning Meeting?* Retrieved from https://www.responsiveclassroom.org/morning-meeting-components

57. Edelman, M. W. (August 8, 2011). Zero Tolerance Discipline Policies: A Failing Idea. *Huff Post Education.* Retrieved from http://www.huffingtonpost.com/marian-wright-edelman/zero-tolerance-discipline_b_919649.html

58. Wilka, J. V. (2011). Analyzing Zero Tolerance School Discipline Policies and Identifying Strategic Opportunities for Intervention. *Harvard Kennedy School.* Retrieved from http://www.childrensdefense.org/library/data/pae-executive-summary.pdf

59. Pacer Center. (2010). *Steps To Take If Your Child Is Being Bullied At School.* Retrieved from http://www.pacer.org/publications/bullypdf/BP-15.pdf

60. Pacer's National Bullying Prevention Center. http://www.pacer.org/bullying/

61. Edutopia Team. (March 16, 2008). Why Integrate Technology into the Cur-

riculum? The Reasons Are Many. *Edutopia.* Retrieved from http://www.edutopia.org/technology-integration-introduction

62. Yednak, C. (n.d.). Tech in your child's elementary school: what to look for, what to ask. *Great Kids!* Retrieved from http://www.greatschools.org/gk/articles/how-technology-is-used-in-elementary-classrooms/

63. Internet Matters. (n.d.). *A parents' guide to tech.* Retrieved from http://www.internetmatters.org/advice/tech-guide/

64. Horrigan, J. B. (April 20, 2015). The numbers behind the broadband 'homework gap'. *Pew Research Center.* Retrieved from http://www.pewresearch.org/fact-tank/2015/04/20/the-numbers-behind-the-broadband-homework-gap/

65. Dobo, N. (June 18, 2015). Poor students often lack a home Internet connection. Is this FCC program a solution? *The Hechinger Report.* Retrieved from http://hechingerreport.org/poor-students-often-lack-a-home-internet-connection-is-this-fcc-program-a-solution/

66. Ibid.

67. Monahan, R. (December 12, 2014). What Happens When Kids Don't Have Internet at Home? *The Atlantic.* Retrieved from http://www.theatlantic.com/education/archive/2014/12/what-happens-when-kids-dont-have-internet-at-home/383680/

68. Morgan, K. (2015). What Are the Pros & Cons of Being Cyberschooled? *Seattle Pi.* Retrieved from http://education.seattlepi.com/pros-cons-being-cyberschooled-3596.html

69. Bandura, A. (1971). *Social Learning Theory.* NY: General Learning Press. Retrieved from http://www.jku.at/org/content/e54521/e54528/e54529/e178059/Bandura_SocialLearningTheory_ger.pdf

70. Morgan, op.cit.

71. CREDO. (April 2011). *Charter School Performance in Pennsylvania.* Retrieved from http://credo.stanford.edu/reports/PA%20State%20Report_20110404_FINAL.pdf

72. Miron, G. and Urschel, J. (July 18, 2012). Understanding and Improving Full-Time Virtual Schools. *NEPC Policy Center.* Retrieved from http://nepc.colorado.edu/publication/understanding-improving-virtual

73. Herald, B. (October 27, 2015). Cyber Charters Have 'Overwhelming Negative Impact,' CREDO Study Finds. *Education Week.* Retrieved from http://mobile.edweek.org/c.jsp?cid=25920011&item=http%3A%2F%2Fapi.edweek.org%2Fv1%2Fblog%2F63%2F%3Fuuid%3D55156

74. Mirel, J. (March 7, 2011). Room for Debate: Discouraging New Teachers. *The New York Times.* Retrieved from http://www.nytimes.com/roomfo.rdebate/2011/03/06/why-blame-the-teachers/discouraging-new-teachers

75. Hanushek, E. and Woessmann, L. (2010). *The High Cost of Low Educational Performance: The Long-Run Impact of Improving PISA Outcomes.* Stanford, CA: Hoover Institution. Retrieved from http://hanushek.stanford.edu/publications/high-cost-low-educational-performance-long-run-impact-improving-pisa-outcomes

76. Chetty, R. Friedman. J. N. and Rockoff, J. (December 2011). The Long Term Impacts of Teacher Value-Added and Student Outcomes in Adulthood. Working Paper 17699. *National Bureau of Economic Research.* Retrieved from http://www.rajchetty.com/chettyfiles/value_added.pdf

77. 77 Lowrey, A. (January 6, 2012). Big Study Links Good Teachers to Lasting Gain. *The New York Times.* Retrieved from http://www.nytimes.com/2012/01/06/education/big-study-links-good-teachers-to-lasting-gain.html?_r=1

78. Ibid.

79. Ibid.

80. Amrein-Beardsley, A. (2014). *Rethinking Value Added Models of Education.* New York: Routledge. P. 210.

81. MET Project (January 2013). Ensuring Fair and Reliable Measures of Effective Teaching. *The Bill and Melinda Gates Foundation.* Retrieved from http://www.edweek.org/media/17teach-met1.pdf

82. Layton, L. (January 9, 2013). Gates Foundation study: We've figured out what makes a good teacher. *The Washington Post.* Retrieved from https://www.washingtonpost.com/national/gates-study-weve-figured-out-what-makes-a-good-teacher/2013/01/08/05ca7d60-59b0-11e2-9fa9-5fbdc9530eb9_story.html

83. Met Study, op.cit.

84. Rothstein, J. And Mathis, W. (January 31, 2013). Review of Two Culminating Reports from the MET Project. *National Education Policy Center.* Retrieved from http://nepc.colorado.edu/thinktank/review-MET-final-2013

85. EQuATE. (February 28, 2011). *Creating a Better System: Recommendations for a Systemic Approach to Improving Educator Effectiveness.* Report to the Governor's Task Force on Teacher Evaluation. Retrieved from https://schoolfinance101.files.wordpress.com/2010/10/equate-report-on-improving-educator-effectiveness-3-1-11.pdf

86. Hanover Research. (February 2013). *Student Perception Surveys and*

Teacher Assessments. Retrieved from http://dese.mo.gov/sites/default/files/Hanover-Research-Student-Surveys.pdf

87. Darling-Hammond, L. (March 24, 2011). Policy Meeting: Teacher Quality Partnerships. *Stanford Center for Opportunity in Education.* Retrieved from https://edpolicy.stanford.edu/events/160

88. Walsh, R. (December 9, 2013). Why Tenure Matters: The Teacher as Advocate and Innovator. *Russ on Reading* blog. Retrieved from http://russonreading.blogspot.com/2013/12/why-tenure-matters-teacher-as-advocate.html

89. Greene, P. (March 25, 2015). Seniority and My Wife. *Education Week.* Retrieved from http://blogs.edweek.org/teachers/view-from-the-cheap-seats/2015/03/from_students_matter_to_campbe.html

90. Winerip, M. (June 5, 2011). Helping Teachers Help Themselves. *The New York Times.* Retrieved from http://www.nytimes.com/2011/06/06/education/06oneducation.html

91. Sommer, C. and Berkshire, J. (February 25, 2014). Internal Documents Reveal Charter Expansion, TFA Go Hand in Hand. *Edushyster* blog. Retrieved from http://edushyster.com/internal-documents-reveal-charter-expansion-tfa-go-hand-in-hand/

92. Shibata, K. (July 29, 2013). Teach for America's Mission to Displace Rank-and-File Educators in Chicago. *In These Times.* Retrieved from http://inthesetimes.com/article/15367/teach_for_americas_mission_to_displace_rank_and_file_educators_in_chicago

93. Donaldson, M.L. and Johnson, S. M. (October 4, 2011). TFA Teachers: How Long Do They Teach? Why Do They Leave? *Education Week.* Retrieved from http://www.edweek.org/ew/articles/2011/10/04/kappan_donaldson.html

94. Ibid.

95. Walsh, R. (November 14, 2014). How to Get a Great Teacher in Every Classroom. *Russ on Reading* blog. Retrieved from http://russonreading.blogspot.com/2014/11/how-to-get-great-teacher-in-every.html

96. Dolgoff, S. (n.d.). 5 Smart Ways to Handle Teacher Troubles. *Parenting.* Retrieved from http://www.parenting.com/article/5-smart-ways-to-handle-teacher-troubles

97. Ibid.

98. Ibid.

99. Common Core State Standards Official Website. http://www.corestandards.

org/about-the-standards/

100. Schneider, M. (April, 23, 2014). Those 24 Common Core 2009 Work Group Members. *Deutsch29* blog. Retrieved from https://deutsch29.wordpress.com/2014/04/23/those-24-common-core-2009-work-group-members/

101. Alliance for Childhood (March 2, 2010). *Joint Statement of Early Childhood Health and Education Professionals on the Common Core Standards Initiative*. Retrieved from http://www.edweek.org/media/joint_statement_on_core_standards.pdf

102. Stotsky, S. (Dec. 11, 2012). Common Core Standards' Devastating Impact on Literary Study and Analytical Thinking. *The Heritage Foundation*. Retrieved from http://www.heritage.org/research/reports/2012/12/questionable-quality-of-the-common-core-english-language-arts-standards

103. Hiebert, E. F. and Van Sluys, K. (2013). Examining Three Assumptions about the Common Core. In Goodman, K., Calfee, R., and Goodman, Y. *Whose Knowledge Counts in Government Literacy Policies?* NY: Routledge.

104. Walsh. R, (May 14, 2013). Does background knowledge matter to reading comprehension? *Russ on Reading* blog. Retrieved from http://russonreading.blogspot.com/2013/05/does-background-knowledge-matter-to.html

105. Rubinstein, Gary. (May 9, 2015). You Reeka Math. *National Education Policy Center.* Retrieved from http://nepc.colorado.edu/blog/you-reeka-math

106. Strauss, V. (Nov. 9, 2013). Why kids are struggling with Common Core Math. *The Washington Post.* Retrieved from https://www.washingtonpost.com/blogs/answer-sheet/wp/2013/11/09/why-young-kids-are-struggling-with-common-core-math/

107. Yatvin, J. (February 27, 2012). A Flawed Approach to Reading in the Common Core Standards. *Education Week.* Retrieved from http://www.edweek.org/ew/articles/2012/02/29/22yatvin.h31.html

108. Thomas, P. L. (May 17, 2015). Power of Common Core Vocabulary Instruction Reaches Back to 1944. *the becoming radical* blog. Retrieved from https://radicalscholarship.wordpress.com/2015/05/17/power-of-common-core-to-reshape-vocabulary-instruction-reaches-back-to-1944/

109. Mathis, W. (2012). Research Based Options for Education Policy: Common Core Standards. *National Education Policy Center.* Retrieved from http://nepc.colorado.edu/files/pb-options-2-commcore-final.pdf

110. Loveless, Tom. (March 18, 2014). A Progress Report on the Common Core. *Brookings.* Retrieved from http://www.brookings.edu/research/reports/2014/03/18-common-core-loveless

111. Zhao, Y. (October 9, 2014). Common Core Side Effects. *Education Week.* Retrieved from http://blogs.edweek.org/edweek/finding_common_ground/2014/10/common_core_side_effects_worth_the_costs.html

112. Effrem, K. (May 27, 2013). The Effect of the Common Core Standards on Teachers and the Teaching Profession. *Education Liberty Watch.* Retrieved from http://edlibertywatch.org/2013/05/the-effect-of-the-common-core-standards-on-teachers-and-the-teaching-profession/

113. National Association for the Education of Young Children. (2005). *NAEYC Early Childhood Program Standards.* Retrieved from http://www.naeyc.org/files/naeyc/Position%20Statement%20EC%20Standards.pdf

114. Merlan, A. (April 29, 2014). Louis CK went on an amazing rant against standardized testing and the common core. *The Village Voice.* Retrieved from http://www.villagevoice.com/news/louis-ck-went-on-an-amazing-twitter-rant-against-standardized-testing-and-the-common-core-6699407

115. Great Schools Partnership. (August 21, 2015). *The Glossary of Education Reform.* Retrieved from http://edglossary.org/standardized-test/

116. The National Center for Fair and Open Testing. (2007*). The Limits of Standardized Tests for Diagnosing and Assisting Student Learning.* Retrieved from http://www.fairtest.org/The+Limits+of+Standardized+Tests

117. Honey, C. (n.d.). For Most Students, Achievement Reflects Income. *School News Network.* Retrieved from http://www.schoolnewsnetwork.org/index.php/2014-15/most-students-achievement-reflects-income/

118. Kohn, A. (January 2001). Fighting the Tests. *Phi Delta Kappan.* Retrieved from http://www.alfiekohn.org/article/fighting-the-tests/

119. The National Center for Fair and Open Testing. (2012). *How Standardized Testing Damages Education.* Retrieved from http://www.fairtest.org/how-standardized-testing-damages-education-pdf

120. Baker, A. (April 30, 2014). Test Prep Endures in New York Schools, Despite Calls to Curb It. *The New York Times.* Retrieved from http://www.nytimes.com/2014/05/01/education/test-prep-endures-in-new-york-schools-despite-calls-to-ease-it.html?_r=0

121. Welner, K. and Mathis, W. (February 12, 2015). Reauthorization of the Elementary and Secondary Education Act: Time to Move Beyond Test-Focused Policies. *National Education Policy Center.* Retrieved from http://nepc.colorado.edu/publication/esea

122. American Statistical Association. (April 8, 2014). *ASA Statement on Using Value-Added Models for Educational Assessment.* Retrieved from https://www.amstat.org/policy/pdfs/ASA_VAM_Statement.pdf

123. Hall-Flavin, D.K. (2014). Is it possible to overcome test anxiety? *The Mayo Clinic.* Retrieved from http://www.mayoclinic.org/diseases-conditions/generalized-anxiety-disorder/expert-answers/test-anxiety/faq-20058195

124. Strauss, V. (February 14, 2014). How 'data walls' in classrooms humiliate kids. *The Washington Post.* Retrieved from https://www.washingtonpost.com/blogs/answer-sheet/wp/2014/02/14/how-data-walls-in-classrooms-can-humiliate-young-kids/

125. Haimson, L. (March 15, 2013). Student education data collecting initiative inBloom puts sensitive information at risk. *The New York Daily News.* Retrieved from http://www.nydailynews.com/new-york/inbloom-education-data-cloud-jeopardizes-lives-new-york-students-article-1.1288189

126. Parent Coalition for School Privacy. (June 22, 2015). *Five Principles to Protect Student Privacy.* Retrieved from http://www.studentprivacymatters.org/five-principles-to-protect-student-data-privacy/

127. Wiggins, G. (2011). A true test: Toward more authentic and equitable assessment. The Kappan, V92 N7 Retrieved from http://www.nisdtx.org/cms/lib/TX21000351/Centricity/Domain/21/j%20carlisle/ATrueTest_Wiggins.pdf

128. Ibid.

129. Kornhaber, M. L. (May 18, 2015). What's Behind the 'Opt Out' Protests Against the Common Core? *Newsweek.* Retrieved from http://www.newsweek.com/whats-behind-opt-out-protests-against-common-core-332560

130. Wallace, K. (April 24, 2015). Parents all over U.S. 'opting out' of standardized student testing. *CNN.* Retrieved from http://www.cnn.com/2015/04/17/living/parents-movement-opt-out-of-testing-feat/

131. Robertson, P. (September 28, 2014). I Refuse to Administer the PARCC. *Peg With Pen.* Retrieved from http://www.pegwithpen.com/2014_09_01_archive.html

132. Hagopian, J. (January 17, 2013). Op-ed: Why Garfield teachers boycotted the MAP test. *The Seattle Times.* Retrieved from http://www.seattletimes.com/opinion/op-ed-why-garfield-teachers-boycotted-the-map-test/

133. Hess, F. M. (May 5, 2015). Opt Out Parents Have a Point. *U. S. News and World Report.* Retrieved from http://www.usnews.com/opinion/knowledge-bank/2015/05/05/parents-opting-out-of-common-core-tests-have-a-point

134. Tyrell, J. and Ebert, M. R. (April 16, 2015). Nearly 65,000 students across LI opt out of state English tests. *Newsday.* Retrieved from http://www.newsday.com/long-island/common-core-testing-on-li-at-least-64-785-students-opt-out-1.10280148

135. Klein, R. (November 18, 2013). 3 People Outraged By Arne Duncan's 'White Suburban Moms' Comment. *The Huffington Post.* Retrieved from http://www.huffingtonpost.com/2013/11/18/arne-duncan-white-moms_n_4297789.html

136. Wall, P. (March 16, 2015). Merryl Tisch: Opting out of the state exams is a 'terrible mistake'. *Chalkbeat New York.* Retrieved from http://ny.chalkbeat.org/2015/03/16/merryl-tisch-opting-out-of-the-state-exams-is-a-terrible-mistake/#.VggBOPlViko

137. Ripley, A. (March 2, 2015). Why stop with vaccines & tests? What else can we opt kids out of? Hamburger gristle? Lice checks? Let's do this people. #optout. Retrieved from https://twitter.com/amandaripley/status/572552002506518528

138. Stewart, C. (April 2, 2015). Painting education the whitest shade of pale. *Citizen Stuart: Public Education for an Educated Public.* Retrieved from http://citizenstewart.org/painting-education-the-whitest-shade-of-pale/

139. Palmer, A. (April 30, 2015). Standardized test backlash: More parents pull kids from exams as protest. *Christian Science Monitor.* Retrieved from http://www.csmonitor.com/USA/Education/2015/0430/Standardized-test-backlash-More-parents-pull-kids-from-exams-as-protest

140. Petrilli, M. et al. (April 28, 2015). Opening minds about closing schools. *Thomas B. Fordham Foundation.* Retrieved from http://edexcellence.net/commentary/podcasts/opening-minds-about-closing-schools

141. Smarick, A. (April 21, 2015). A test of education reform. *Common Core Watch.* Retrieved from http://edexcellence.net/articles/a-test-of-education-reform

142. Greene, Peter. (March 4, 2015). Your Granular Achievement Report. *Curmudgucation* blog. Retrieved from http://www.curmudgucation.blogspot.com/

143. Walsh, R. (April 18, 2014). Attention, Not Retention. *Russ on Reading* blog. Retrieved from http://russonreading.blogspot.com/2014/04/attention-not-retention.html

144. Strauss, V. (April 2, 2015). Will schools lose federal funds if kids don't take mandated tests? Fact vs. threat. *The Washington Post.* Retrieved from https://www.washingtonpost.com/blogs/answer-sheet/wp/2015/04/02/will-schools-lose-federal-funds-if-kids-dont-take-mandated-tests-fact-vs-threat/

145. Ravitch, D. (April 26, 2015). Speech given before the Network for Public Education Conference, Chicago, IL.

146. Strauss, V. (April 7, 2015). How the Obamas opted their children out of

high-stakes standardized tests. *The Washington Post.* Retrieved from https://www.washingtonpost.com/blogs/answer-sheet/wp/2015/04/07/how-the-obamas-opted-their-children-out-of-high-stakes-standardized-tests/

147. National Alliance for Carter Schools. (n.d.). *What are public charter schools?* Retrieved from http://www.publiccharters.org/get-the-facts/public-charter-schools/

148. Kahlenberg, K. D. and Potter, H. (August 30, 2014). The original charter school vision. *The New York Times.* Retrieved from http://www.nytimes.com/2014/08/31/opinion/sunday/albert-shanker-the-original-charter-school-visionary.html?_r=2

149. Ravitch, D. (2013). *Reign of Error: The Hoax of the Privatization Movement and the Danger to America's Public Schools.* New York: Knopf

150. Greene, Peter. (July 8, 2014). How to Properly Cash in on the Charter School Movement. *The Huffington Post.* Retrieved from http://www.huffingtonpost.com/peter-greene/charter-schools-money_b_5287499.html

151. Jersey Jazzman blog. (November 29, 2013). *Why reform is really union busting.* Retrieved from http://jerseyjazzman.blogspot.com/2013/11/when-reform-is-really-union-busting.html

152. Berliner, D. and Glass, G. (2014). *50 Myths and Lies that Threaten America's Public Schools.* New York: Teachers College Press.

153. Ravitch, D. (October 9, 2013). Charter Schools Insist: We Are Not Public Schools. *Diane Ravitch's blog.* Retrieved from http://dianeravitch.net/2013/10/09/charter-schools-insist-we-are-private-not-public/

154. Smith, G. B. (March 14, 2014). Judge rules that state Controller Thomas DiNapoli cannot audit charter schools. *The New York Daily News.* Retrieved from http://www.nydailynews.com/new-york/education/state-comptroller-audit-charter-schools-judge-article-1.1721265

155. Bryant, J. (October 2, 2014). The great charter school rip-off: Finally, the truth catches up to education "reform" phonies. *Salon.* Retrieved from http://www.salon.com/2014/10/02/the_great_charter_school_rip_off_finally_the_truth_catches_up_to_education_reform_phonies/

156. Livingstone, D. (May 30, 2015). Charter schools misspend millions of Ohio tax dollars as efforts to police them are privatized. *Ohio.com.* Retrieved from http://www.ohio.com/news/local/charter-schools-misspend-millions-of-ohio-tax-dollars-as-efforts-to-police-them-are-privatized-1.596318

157. The Center for Popular Democracy. (April 2015). *The Tip of the Iceberg: Charter School Vulnerabilities to Waste, Fraud, And Abuse.* Retrieved from http://populardemocracy.org/news/tip-iceberg-charter-school-vulnerabilities-waste-fraud-and-abuse

158. KIPP.org (n.d.) *How we do it.* Retrieved from http://www.kipp.org/our-approach/five-pillars

159. Taylor, K. (April 6, 2015). At Success Academy Charter Schools, High Scores and Polarizing Tactics. *The New York Times.* Retrieved from http://www.nytimes.com/2015/04/07/nyregion/at-success-academy-charter-schools-polarizing-methods-and-superior-results.html

160. Pelto, J. (October 4, 2013). Child Abuse in the form of the "No Excuses" education model. *Wait What?* blog. Retrieved from http://jonathanpelto.com/2013/10/04/child-abuse-form-excuses-education-model/

161. Walsh, R. (October 6, 2013). Colonialism in the Inner City. *Russ on Reading* blog. Retrieved from http://russonreading.blogspot.com/2013/10/colonialism-in-inner-city-charter_6.html

162. Strauss, V. (February 14, 2014). How 'data walls' in classrooms humiliate kids. *The Washington Post.* Retrieved from https://www.washingtonpost.com/blogs/answer-sheet/wp/2014/02/14/how-data-walls-in-classrooms-can-humiliate-young-kids/

163. The Oklahoman Editorial Board. (March 27, 2013). KIPP provides an educational model worth emulating. *NewsOK.* Retrieved from http://newsok.com/kipp-provides-an-educational-model-worth-emulating/article/3771508

164. Lips, D. (January 12, 2010). How Online Learning Is Revolutionizing K-12 Education and Benefiting Students. *The Heritage Foundation.* Retrieved from http://www.heritage.org/research/reports/2010/01/how-online-learning-is-revolutionizing-k12-education-and-benefiting-students

165. Maul, A. (April 27, 2015). Review of Urban Charter School Study 2015. *National Education Policy Center.* Retrieved from http://nepc.colorado.edu/thinktank/review-urban-charter-school

166. Manno, M. (August 9, 2012). The Pros and Cons of Merit Based Pay for Teachers. *Teach* blog. Retrieved from http://teach.com/education-policy/the-pros-and-cons-of-merit-based-pay-for-teachers

167. Hull, J. (n.d.). How do charter schools compare to traditional public schools in student performance? *Data First.* Retrieved from http://www.data-first.org/questions/how-do-charter-schools-compare-to-regular-public-schools-in-student-performance/

168. Ozimek, A. (January 11, 2015). The Unappreciated Success of Charter Schools. *Forbes.* Retrieved from http://www.forbes.com/sites/modeled-behavior/2015/01/11/charter-success/

169. Maul, A. (April 27, 2015). Review of Urban Charter School Study 2015. National Education Policy Center. Retrieved from http://nepc.colorado.

edu/thinktank/review-urban-charter-school

170. Hornbeck, D. (February 27, 2015). Charter schools do not equal education reform. *The Baltimore Sun.* Retrieved from http://www.baltimoresun.com/news/opinion/oped/bs-ed-hornbeck-charters-20150301-story.html

171. Global Credit Research. (October 15, 2013). Moody's: Charter schools pose greatest credit challenge to school districts in economically weak urban areas. *Moody's Investor Service.* Retrieved from https://www.moodys.com/research/Moodys-Charter-schools-pose-greatest-credit-challenge-to-school-districts--PR_284505?WT.mc_id=NLTITLE_YYYYMMDD_PR_284505%3C%2fp%3E

172. Welner, K.G. (April 22, 2013). The Dirty Dozen: How Charter Schools Influence Student Enrollment. *Teachers College Record.* Retrieved from http://www.tcrecord.org/content.asp?contentid=17104

173. Hornbeck, op cit.

174. DiCarlo M. (April 9, 2015). Teacher Turnover at Success Academy Charter Schools. *Albert Shanker Institute.* Retrieved from http://www.shankerinstitute.org/blog/teacher-turnover-success-academy-charter-schools

175. Sawchuck, S. (April 13, 2015). N.Y. Budget Accord Seeks to Tighten Rules on Teacher Quality. *Education Week.* 34(27), 6. Retrieved from http://www.edweek.org/ew/articles/2015/04/15/ny-budget-accord-seeks-to-tighten-rules.html

176. Hornbeck, op cit.

177. Zeehandalaar. D. and Northern, A. M. (August 26, 2013). What Parents Want: Education Preferences and Trade-offs. *Thomas B. Fordham Institute.* Retrieved from http://edexcellence.net/publications/what-parents-want.html

178. Friedman Foundation for Educational Choice (2003). *Milton Friedman on Vouchers.* Retrieved from http://www.edchoice.org/who-we-are/our-founders/the-friedmans-on-school-choice/article/milton-friedman-on-vouchers/

179. Save Our Schools New Jersey. (2015). *School Voucher Basics.* Retrieved from http://www.saveourschoolsnj.org/vouchers/

180. Center for Education Reform. (2014). *School Choice Today: Voucher Laws Across the States.* Retrieved from https://www.edreform.com/wp-content/uploads/2014/08/VoucherRankings-Report5.pdf

181. Americans United for Separation of Church and State. (February 2011). *10 Reasons Why Private School Vouchers Should Be Rejected.* Retrieved from https://www.au.org/church-state/february-2011-church-state/featured/10-

reasons-why-private-school-vouchers-should-be#sthash.MZqzhRL8.dpuf

182. Hiltzik, M. (August 22, 2014). The case against school vouchers in one blistering court ruling. *The Los Angeles Times.* Retrieved from http://www.latimes.com/business/hiltzik/la-fi-mh-all-thats-wrong-with-school-vouchers-20140822-column.html

183. Ibid.

184. Richards, E. (March 30, 2011). Voucher data takes a new twist. *Milwaukee Journal Sentinel.* Retrieved from http://www.jsonline.com/news/education/118886284.html

185. Richards, E. and Crow, K. April 8, 2014). Voucher students post gain in math, reading; still lag public schools. *Milwaukee Journal Sentinel.* Retrieved from http://www.jsonline.com/news/education/voucher-students-post-gain-in-math-reading-still-lag-public-schools-b99243092z1-254382141.html

186. University of Arkansas Department of Education Reform. (February 1, 2012). *Milwaukee Parental Choice Program Evaluation.* Retrieved from http://www.uaedreform.org/milwaukee-parental-choice-program-evaluation/

187. Stein, J. and Manley, P. (February 3, 2015). Walker's budget expands school vouchers, holds line on taxes. *Milwaukee Journal Sentinel.* Retrieved from http://www.jsonline.com/news/statepolitics/walkers-budget-will-address-shortfall-education-roads-and-arena-b99438453z1-290687071.html

188. Huff Post Education. (June 1, 2011). School Vouchers Under The Microscope: Do They Really Improve Student Achievement? *The Huffington Post.* Retrieved from http://www.huffingtonpost.com/2011/04/01/school-vouchers-education-reform_n_843861.html

189. Statement of Administration Policy. (March 29, 2011*). H.R. 471 – Scholarships for Opportunity and Results Act.* Retrieved from https://www.whitehouse.gov/sites/default/files/omb/legislative/sap/112/saphr471h_20110329.pdf

190. Berkshire, J. (June 20, 2015). Backpacks Full of Cash. *Edushyster* blog. Retrieved from http://edushyster.com/backpacks-full-of-cash/

191. Wetzel, J. (2012). Homeschooling goes under the microscope in new Peabody research. *Research News at Vanderbilt.* Retrieved from http://news.vanderbilt.edu/2012/11/homeschooling/

192. Home Schooling Legal Defense Association (HSLDA). https://www.hslda.org/laws/

193. Ibid.

194. Coalition for Responsible Home Education. (n. d.). *Homeschooling & Educational Neglect.* Retrieved from http://www.responsiblehomeschooling.org/policy-issues/abuse-and-neglect/educational-neglect/

Acknowledgements

This book was made possible by the great teacher, writer, researcher and advocate for social justice, Denny Taylor. Thirty-years ago, while in graduate school, I read the seminal book on literacy in the home, Denny's *Family Literacy: Young Children Learn to Read and Write.* It was one of those life-changing books. I am forever grateful that all these years later Denny saw the need for this present book and had the confidence in me to write it.

Darcie Cimirusti, parent, blogger and public education advocate without peer, helped formulate the outline that eventually became this book. Thanks also to Bruce Ingraham, Don Stoll, Pete Rosenberg, and Leonard Alborn, my friends near and far who read chapters of the book and made invaluable suggestions that have made this book better, and who also offered much appreciated support along the way. Bob Krech, my colleague, friend and the best math teacher I ever met, offered great insights for the section on mathematics teaching and learning.

Education historian Diane Ravitch reposted several of my blog entries from *Russ on Reading* and helped me immeasurably in gaining the wider audience that led to the invitation to write this book. Jonathan Pelto, of the *Wait, What?* blog, was extraordinarily generous in introducing me to the wider world of education bloggers through the Education Bloggers Network. Carol Burris, award winning principal and hero of public education, has been an early and frequent sharer of my work. Other education bloggers have also been invaluable to me as I continued my education in the new world of education reform. Thanks especially to Peter Greene, P. L. Thomas, Deborah Meier, Anthony Cody, Valerie Strauss, Nancy Flanagan, "Jersey Jazzman" Bruce Weber, Mercedes Schneider, Bruce Baker, Julie Larrea Borst, "Edushyster" Jennifer Berkshire, Steven Singer, Susan DuFresne, Dora Taylor, John Thompson and Ani McHugh.

Thanks also to my children Beth Rainville, Megan Stewart and Bruce Walsh for their encouragement, understanding and belief. I learned so much of what is contained in these pages from watching you grow into the wonderful adults you are. Finally, and most indispensably, thanks to my wife, Cindy Mershon, a great teacher of literacy, a fine writer and editor, a sympathetic ear and sometimes critical eye when I need one, and my partner in life, laughter, learning and love.

About the Author: Russ Walsh

Russ Walsh has had a 45 year career in public education as a teacher, literacy specialist, curriculum supervisor and college instructor. He is currently the Coordinator of College Reading at Rider University.

After beginning his career as a history teacher, Russ switched gears, earned a degree in literacy, and then worked for much of his career in the literacy field, including stints as an elementary reading specialist and a literacy supervisor. He has taught every level from kindergarten through graduate school. His major academic interests have been instructional practice and parental involvement in education.

Russ was active for many years with the International Literacy Association (ILA) as a member of the Parents and Reading Committee, as well as co-founder and chair of the Parents and Reading Special Interest Group. Russ helped organize and deliver parent programs as a part of ILA's yearly international conference. He has presented hundreds of workshops and papers for parents and teachers at local, regional, national and international conferences.

Russ blogs on public education, literacy instruction and teaching practice at *Russ on Reading*. He lives in Bucks County, Pennsylvania with his wife, Cindy Mershon, and their three cocker spaniels.

Made in the USA
Middletown, DE
24 December 2017